First-Rate Reading™

Literature-Based Activities that Support Research-Based Instruction

by **E**lizabeth Suarez Aguerre

Grade 3

Carson-Dellosa Publishing Company, Inc.
Greensboro, North Carolina

Credits

to *First-Rate Reading*™

Project Coordinator: Kelly Gunzenhauser

Editors: Ellen Holmes and Donna Walkush

Layout Designer: Jon Nawrocik

Cover Designer: Annette Hollister-Papp

Cover Illustrator: Bill Neville

Illustrators: Bill Neville and Wayne Miller

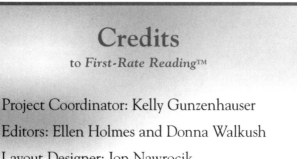

Dedication

of *First-Rate Reading*™

To Mami and Papi for everything, and to Xiomi for always letting me borrow her typewriter when I was little.

ISBN 0-88724-252-9

Table of Contents
to *First-Rate Reading*™

Introduction
to *First-Rate Reading*™

• *What is Put Reading First?*
By now, most educators are familiar with the Put Reading First federal initiative. Part of the No Child Left Behind Act, Reading First is the culmination of research designed to identify best practices for reading teachers. Reading First holds teachers accountable for students' mastery of five very specific components of literacy: phonemic awareness, phonics, fluency, vocabulary, and comprehension. Practices that focus on these components are already in use by many teachers, and several states have received grants to implement Reading First programs.

• *How will the* First-Rate Reading™ *series help me teach reading?*
In addition to the fact that literacy is a basic and necessary skill, the love of books and the desire to share that love inspires many teachers. Even in the face of increased standardized testing and skill-based instruction, fine children's literature continues to be an important part of reading curriculums. This series helps teachers connect great literature with lessons that reinforce the components of Reading First by:
   • providing additional phonemic awareness and phonics practice for students who need it
   • reinforcing phonics concepts with activities that conform to an existing, sequential phonics program
   • making teaching vocabulary strategies fun and relevant
   • creating opportunities for students to practice fluency skills with age-appropriate texts
   • engaging students in discussions and activities that help them comprehend what they read and apply those meanings to other literature and to their own lives

• *Why were these children's books chosen for this series?*
Teaching reading is much easier when students (and teachers) have a desire to read. These books were chosen because students respond to real, excellent literature (many are Caldecott Medal and Newbery Medal winners), and because they are student and teacher favorites. Attention is paid to old favorites, such as *Green Eggs and Ham* and *Frog and Toad Together,* as well as modern classics like *If You Take a Mouse to School* and *Because of Winn-Dixie.* There is truly something for every reader to enjoy.

• *Some activities and reproducibles seem very advanced/very easy for my class. How do I adjust them to fit different levels?*
After completing beginning-of-the-year assessments, you should have an idea of students' reading and writing skills. What may take longer to assess is their different abilities to work independently. At the third-grade level, you should direct the more difficult activities by doing them in whole-class, small-group, or partner settings. Additionally, make the more complicated reproducibles accessible by modeling what students should do, reading all words and directions aloud to them, saying the names of pictures and the sounds of letters, etc. For activities which require students to write, consider having students write drafts of their work on separate sheets of paper, then copy their corrected work onto reproducibles for publishing. Also, consider having students color every page on which there is art, both to give them extra fine-motor-skill practice and to let them make the work "their own."

- *How do I actually use the children's books with the activities?*

Some activities use the actual text from the books, while others use themes that are similar to those in the books. For example, a phonics activity based around *Charlotte's Web* looks at the ch digraph, with Charlotte as the example. Other activities for *Charlotte's Web* use the argument between Fern and her Father about Wilbur as the basis for a lesson about tone, and the theme of friendship for a journal topic. Page numbers in each children's book are referenced, but bear in mind that some books do not have page numbers, and that numbering may change according to which edition you use.

- *How do I match these activities to the phonics system I have to follow, and how do I know when to choose which lesson?*

In the Table of Contents, all of the activities are listed by type. Some of the activities are general in what they teach (making predictions, alphabet practice, etc.) but are unique in how they are executed. Other activities are very specific in what they teach (/g/ sounds, ot word family, etc.). Since most beginning reading programs are driven by the order in which phonemic awareness and phonics elements are taught, it may be most convenient to refer to the Phonemic Awareness and Phonics key below, and base literature choices on how your program's phonics lessons correspond to the phonics key below.

Phonemic Awareness/Phonics
Key Page References

short /a/–28, 118
long /a/–10, 28, 78, 80, 118
/al/ as in tall–118
au/aw–18
/c/ (hard and soft)–48, 50
long /e/ (ie and y)–20
silent e–20
ear sounds–20
/g/ (hard and soft)–60, 78, 80
silent gh, ght–108, 110
j–60
silent l–110
short /o/–28, 90
long /o/–90
/oo/–48, 68
ou/ow–18
p–100
qu–108, 150
r-controlled vowels–28, 68, 90, 138
long /u/–48
silent w–80
x(/ks/)–30
y–30, 70

alliteration–98
alphabetizing–110, 140
blending, counting, or isolating phonemes–8, 88, 128, 148
consonant blends–48, 90, 118
consonant digraphs–38, 40, 50, 78, 128, 130
consonants (voiced and unvoiced)–58, 128
initial phonemes–148
letter names–38
making words–70
onsets and rimes–60
phoneme sorting–98
phonemic awareness practice–8, 58, 68, 118, 138, 148
phonics assessment–30
phonics practice–10, 50, 120, 140
phonics rules for adding endings–100
rhymes (words, word families, phonemes)–38, 40, 58, 60, 128
sound spelling–140
sound words–8, 18, 98, 108, 148
spelling with manipulatives–40
syllable work–18, 100, 138
tactile writing–130
vowel teams–10, 120, 150

Pronunciation Guide

to *First-Rate Reading*™

This book uses very simple descriptions of sounds in order to make the activities easily adaptable to your school's phonics program. These guidelines are not meant to be a full phonics program. In **every** case, use the phoneme and phonics cues that your phonics program recommends. See the chart below for specific information about the sounds presented in this series.

Vowel Sounds

These symbols encompass the sounds made by each combination of vowels and consonants. The letter combinations are paired with example words that make the sounds.

short /a/ and long /a/ • long /a/ includes ai as in rain, a_e as in cake, and ea as in break

short /e/ and long /e/ • short /e/ includes ea as in breath
   • long /e/ includes ea as in steal, ee as in steel, ei as in either, ie as in thief, and y as in happy

short /i/ and long /i/ • short /i/ includes y as in myth (Note: some phonics programs deem ing as short /i/)
   • long /i/ includes ie as in tried, i_e as in ice, igh as in high, ight as in night, and y as in my

short /o/ and long /o/ • long /o/ includes oa as in goat, o_e as in role, ou as in soul, and ow as in slow

short /u/ and long /u/ • short /u/ includes oo as in blood
   • long /u/ may include ew as in few, ou as in youth, ue as in blue, oo as in scoot (Different phonics programs consider either /yu/ and/or /oo/ as long /u/)

Vowel Combinations, Vowel Teams, and Vowel-Consonant Teams

Difficult vowel combinations are treated individually. Each is paired with an example word that makes the sound.

- /au/ as in caught
- /oi/ and /oy/ as in poise and joy
- /ou/ and /ow/ as in loud and cow
- /aw/ as in saw (/au/ and /aw/ may differ depending on regional dialect
- /oo/ as in spoon, foot, or short /u/ as in blood

R-Controlled Vowels and Diphthongs

Rather than substitute the *schwa* character (ə) for r-controlled vowels and diphthongs, they are listed with example words. This helps remind teachers to differentiate, for example, between the /or/ sound in the word *for* and the /or/ sound in the word *doctor*, so that students don't over-pronounce the *or* as doctOR or the *or* in *for* as *fur*. Additionally, many students who are learning to read find the schwa confusing in print and will learn the correct local pronunciation without additional coaching.

Consonant Sounds

/b/	/d/	/f/	/g/ (hard g as in goat)	/h/
/j/ (soft g as in gem)	/k/ (hard c as in cat)	/l/	/m/	/n/
/p/	/kw/ (for q with u)	/r/	/s/ (soft c as in cell)	/t/
/v/	/w/	/ks/ (x as in fox)	/y/	/z/

Digraphs

/ch/   /sh/ (ss as in mission, ch as in machine)   /th/ as in this (not voiced)
/th/ as in then (voiced)   /wh/ as in whale   /zh/ as in vision

Amber Brown Is Not a Crayon

by Paula Danziger

(G. P. Putnam's Sons, 1994)

Justin Daniels and Amber Brown do everything together. Now that Justin is moving to Alabama with his family, neither Amber nor Justin knows how to handle the situation. Although the story is written from Amber's perspective, it also depicts Justin's feelings and fears.

Related books by Paula Danziger: *Amber Brown Goes Fourth* (Putnam, 1995); *Amber Brown Is Feeling Blue* (Putnam, 1998); *You Can't Eat Your Chicken Pox, Amber Brown* (Putnam, 1995)

Phonemic Awareness Activities
for *Amber Brown is Not a Crayon*

Pre-reading Activity: Provide students with a chance to practice and review many phonemic skills. Read the book title to students. Repeat the word *Amber* and ask students to count the phonemes. Remind students that phonemes are not the same as syllables—phonemes are the different sounds in words. (Students may think that the final two letters in *Amber* make up two phonemes.) Say *Amber* again, pausing between each sound (/a/, /m/, /b/, /er/). After students have correctly identified the number of phonemes in *Amber*, repeat with the word *Brown*. Again, help students identify that /ow/ is a diphthong created by the letters o and w. Help students count the four phonemes in Brown (/b/, /r/, /ow/, /n/). Review consonant blends if necessary.

During-reading Activity: In chapter 1, page 7, pause to discuss how Justin makes noises to give clues to Amber about what he "is" at that moment, such as when he "tick tocks" to be an alarm clock, then says "Bzzzzzz. Squawk." when he is a "cuckoo bird alarm clock" with his "tail feathers" caught. In chapter 4, note when Justin "ka-thwonks" to pretend to be a hopping kangaroo. Tell students that they will be making up, reading, and writing sounds. Copy the Silly Sounds reproducible (page 9) and pair students. Have pairs fill in the blanks by providing either the objects, the sounds, or both. After students finish, let them share responses and compare answers. Give groups a chance to make their created sounds so the class can guess, like Amber would for Justin.

Post-reading Activity: Reinforce specific phonemic skills according to your students' needs. Give each small group a set of blank index cards. Assign each group a "secret" phonemic pattern to find in the book. For example, have a group look for words in the book that have consonant digraphs, or the sounds of /e/, or other patterns on which students need review. On the index cards, direct groups to list words that follow the assigned phonemic patterns. After groups have finished finding words, have groups present their word cards to the class. Then, let the class guess what phonemic pattern the words have in common.

Silly Sounds

phonemic awareness reproducible for
Amber Brown Is Not a Crayon

Names _____ Date _____

Read the descriptions and sounds below. When a sound is written for you, sound out and say the word. Then, write something that might make that sound. When an object description is provided, think of a sound it might make, say the sound, then write that sound. Fill in the last blanks with your own sounds and ideas—like Justin! An example has been done for you.

Object: a frog jumping into a
       muddy pond
Sound: Blupp!

Object: a little kid blowing bubbles into his
       milk through a straw
Sound: _____

Object: a puppy running around with an
       empty tin can stuck on one paw
Sound: _____

Object: _____
       _____
Sound: Kawoosh! Kawoosh!

Object: _____
       _____
Sound: Scree! Scree! Scree!

Object: _____
       _____
Sound: _____

Object: _____
       _____
Sound: _____

Object: _____
       _____
Sound: _____

Phonics Activities
for *Amber Brown Is Not a Crayon*

re-reading Activity: Show students the title *Amber Brown Is Not a Crayon* and ask them to identify all of the sounds the vowels make in the words. Point out how the long /a/ sound in *crayon* is represented by the vowel digraph ay. Explain that the long /a/ sound can be written a number of ways. Write the following words on the board: *play, brain, blame, rain, sway, lake.* Ask students what letters make the long /a/ sound in each word (ay, ai, a_e). Write the following words and phrases on the board, replacing specific letters with blanks: *pl_ne, third gr_der, picture d__, moving aw__, n_me, pl__, r__se your hand, expl__n, w__ting for him to s__ he'll miss me, unb_ked brownie mix, I want you to st__.* Tell students that these are words and phrases from the book and that some of the letters are missing. Have students guess what the words and phrases are by replacing the letters that make the long /a/ sound in each. Then, call on students to fill in the missing letters. Encourage students to look for these words and phrases as they read the book.

uring-reading Activity: After reading chapter 2, reread the excerpt when Amber comments on what a great team she and Justin are: "Justin, on the other hand, is very neat about pasting things. My handwriting is much better. Another example of what a great team we are." (*Amber Brown Is Not a Crayon*, page 16). Write the words *great team* on the board and have students list some of the other examples mentioned in the book that make Amber and Justin a great team. Then, tell students that the letters e and a are also a "great team." Explain that when two vowels are together in a word, they are called a *vowel team.* Ask students to notice what sound the ea team makes in the word *great.* Then, have students notice what sound ea makes in the word *team.* Tell students that the vowel team ea almost always makes the long /e/ sound, as in *team, meat, breathe,* and *leave*—about 74% of the time. The ea also makes the short /e/ sound, as in *sweat, bread,* and *head,* about 25% of the time. The other 1% of the time, ea makes the long /a/ sound, as in *great, steak,* and *break.* Challenge students to see if this is true by listing words containing the ea vowel team as they find them during reading. Have students use the Great Team! reproducible (page 11) to record words that contain ea as students encounter them in the book. After completing the book, count up the total number per category (long /a/, long /e/, short /e/) and compare to see if the numbers match the statistics.

ost-reading Activity: The title of the book, *Amber Brown Is Not a Crayon*, refers to the fact that some people make fun of the lead character's name. Write the name *Amber* on the board. What phonics characteristics do students notice about it? (It has a short /a/ sound, an r-controlled e, two syllables, four phonemes, etc.) Write *Justin* on the board and list its phonics characteristics. (It has a short /u/ and /i/, the st blend, two syllables, etc.) Let each student write her name at the top of a piece of paper. At the bottom, have her write phonics characteristics of her name. Then, ask students to fold their papers and tear them in half horizontally. Collect the phonics characteristics half sheets and distribute them randomly. Allow students time to guess names that match the phonics characteristics they receive.

Great Team!

phonics reproducible for
Amber Brown Is Not a Crayon

Name_____ Date_____

Amber and Justin make a great team, just like the ea vowel team! While reading the book, use this sheet to record words you find that contain the ea vowel team. Write each word in the correct column.

Long /a/ as in *great*	Long /e/ as in *team*	Short /e/ as in *bread*
_____	_____	_____
_____	_____	_____
_____	_____	_____
_____	_____	_____
_____	_____	_____
_____	_____	_____
_____	_____	_____
_____	_____	_____
_____	_____	_____
_____	_____	_____
_____	_____	_____
_____	_____	_____
_____	_____	_____
_____	_____	_____
_____	_____	_____
_____	_____	_____

Vocabulary Activities
for *Amber Brown Is Not a Crayon*

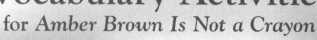re-reading Activity: Read the title to students and ask them why they think the book is called *Amber Brown Is Not a Crayon*. Why would she have to say she is not a crayon? What would make someone think she is? Ask a student to look up the word *amber* in a dictionary. Discuss that amber is a shade of the color brown. Tell students that when they begin reading, they will find sections in the book where Amber is teased because of her name. Tell students that the words *amber* and *brown* are synonyms because they both mean the same thing. (Some dictionaries call *amber* yellow.) Tell students that authors often use "more interesting" or "fancier" words for colors instead of *brown, red, black,* etc. Ask students what other words they might use for the color brown such as *chocolate, tan,* etc. Allow students to look through clothing or home furnishings catalogs for ideas. Give each student a copy of the "Colorful Words" reproducible (page 13). Read some of the color synonyms and discuss the power of using one word instead of another in writing. Write a sentence using one of the "basic" color words such as *The ocean was blue.* Then, have students refer to their sheets to rewrite the sentence using a more "colorful" color word such as *The ocean was azure.* Discuss which sentence sounds more interesting, beautiful, poetic, descriptive, etc. Have each student write a sentence for each color word on her sheet using one of the synonyms listed. Then, give students an opportunity to share their sentences. Have students keep their reproducibles to use as reference for future writing activities.

uring-reading Activity: While reading chapter 2, pause after reading page 15 (Justin's postcard to his brother and Amber's comments about it). Write the two words *bare* and *bear* on the board. Tell students that Justin's spelling mistake is a very common one. Many people get confused when writing words such as these because the words sound exactly the same, but they are spelled differently and mean different things. Tell students that these words are called *homophones* or *homonyms*. (The word *homophone* reminds students that they could "hear" a person talking on a "phone," and when you "hear" two homophones, they sound alike.) List the following homophones on the board: *ate/eight, be/bee, dear/deer, flower/flour, red/read, sea/see, to/too/two.* Have students use each word correctly in a sentence. Have students brainstorm other homophones, or present students with a word and definition and have them think of its matching homophone. After compiling a list, give students index cards and have them copy each homophone on a card. Have students add simple drawings to the cards to provide clues about the words' meanings. Then, have students use the cards to play a matching game in pairs or independently.

ost-reading Activity: Have students go back through the book to find when Amber refers to herself as "I, Amber Brown. . . ." Ask students why they think the author chose to write that way (to help the reader "hear" Amber's "voice," to give Amber more personality, to show the reader that Amber is narrating the story, etc.). Tell students that the word *I* is a pronoun and that a pronoun, such as my, ours, us, you, he, etc., is a word that replaces the name of a noun. Have students skim through the book to find other pronouns. Compile a list on the board. As you list each pronoun, ask students who or what that pronoun is referring to and write the noun next to it. For example, write *Justin* next to *he,* *Amber* next to *her,* etc.

Colorful Words

vocabulary reproducible for

Amber Brown Is Not a Crayon

Name_____ Date_____

Good writers use interesting language. This list of color synonyms will help you do that!
Use this sheet as a reference for writing activities.

black   ebony, jet, night, raven, sable, soot

blue   aquamarine, azure, cobalt blue, cyan, indigo, midnight blue, royal blue, sapphire, turquoise

brown   amber, auburn, bronze, chestnut, chocolate, coffee, mahogany, nutmeg, tan

gray   aluminum, charcoal, silver, steel

green   celadon, emerald green, forest, grass green, jade, kelly green, mint green, moss green, pea green, olive

orange   burnt sienna, peach, persimmon, pumpkin, salmon, tangerine, terra-cotta

purple   burgundy, eggplant, grape, lavender, lilac, magenta, mauve, violet, wine

red   cherry, crimson, garnet, maroon, poppy, rose, vermilion, wine

white   cream, ecru, eggshell, ivory, linen, pearl, snow

yellow   amber, buff, canary yellow, gold, lemon yellow, maize, sand, sunflower

Fluency Activities

for *Amber Brown Is Not a Crayon*

Pre-reading Activity: Read the title aloud. Ask students, "Did you hear how I grouped the words *Amber* and *Brown* together? That makes sense because they are her first and last names. It would not sound right if I said Amber [pause] Brown is not a [pause] crayon." Remind students that this is called "chunking" because you are putting together chunks or groups of words. Ask students what other words might be chunked when reading the title aloud. (*Is* and *not* would probably be chunked together, also.)

During-reading Activity: While you are reading, pause to point out "clues" the author provides that help you read more fluently and expressively. For example, point out when Amber says "WHAT are you doing?" (*Amber Brown Is Not a Crayon*, page 32) to Justin, and Hannah says "SOOOOOO immature" (*Amber Brown Is Not a Crayon*, page 36) to Amber and Justin. Reread these sentences, and have students repeat them, stressing the word *what* and extending the *so*. Discuss why the author chose to write these words in this way. Also, pause after reading in chapter 5 when Amber says "'Yea. Exciting,' I say, in what my mother calls 'Little Ms. Amber's sarcastic voice.'" Discuss how Amber might sound when she is being sarcastic and have students read the line using sarcastic voices. Have students volunteer to reread the same line using normal voices, sincerely excited voices, etc. Discuss the differences between the voices and how reading something in the same manner as a character affects fluency and thus, comprehension. Repeat this discussion after reading "Mr. Cohen uses his teacher 'cut it out' voice." in chapter 6. Have students discuss what the author meant by this. What does a teacher sound like when he wants you to "cut it out?" Students will probably imitate you!

Post-reading Activity: Reread page 12 in the book when the class "flies" to China and writes postcards to friends and family. If possible, simulate a flight to China (or other destination) as Mr. Cohen does in the book. Show a video about the destination when you "arrive," or use photos and information from the Internet. Then, direct each student to write a postcard to someone. Distribute a copy of the Wish You Were Here! reproducible (page 15) to each student. Have students write postcards, then give students an opportunity to practice reading their postcards aloud. Remind students that fluent readers pause at appropriate places, read smoothly and naturally, and sound the way a person would usually sound while speaking. Also, remind them that they are on vacation. Are they having a terrific time? A terrible time? Their voices should reflect the experiences written on the postcards. Encourage students to reread their postcards about four times before sharing with the class. Praise fluent readers and provide specific feedback for those who are still developing.

fluency reproducible for

Amber Brown Is Not a Crayon

Name_____ Date_____

Pretend you are visiting a far-away place. Write a postcard to someone. Tell about good and bad experiences—maybe you like where you are and maybe you don't! Practice reading your postcard and be prepared to read the postcard to the class.

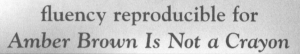

Comprehension Activities
for *Amber Brown Is Not a Crayon*

Pre-reading Activity: Help students realize how they can "prepare their brains" before reading a book in order to aid their comprehension. Place the following items in a box or bag: a brown crayon, a passport (or fake one), a toy plane or picture of a plane, gum, a fortune cookie, an Oreo® cookie, a For Sale sign, and a map of Alabama. Tell students that you have collected a few items that have to do with the book they will be reading and that their job will be to use the items as clues to form some predictions about the book. Give each student a copy of the Plot Predictions reproducible (page 17). (If you want students to make predictions about more than three objects, make double-sided copies, or make a transparency for the overhead and let students copy the format.) Before showing students the cover or title of the book, show them each item, and have them write its name on the first blanks. Then, have students write short predictions about what the item will have to do with the story's plot. Point out to students how difficult this is when you have no idea about the book—it's basically a "wild guess." Next, show students the cover of the book, and read the title and the blurb on the back. Have them write new predictions for each item shown. Point out to students how much easier this is now that they have previewed the book. Have students put the reproducibles away as you read the book, but ask them to keep their predictions in mind as they read. As a final step, have students add new, more specific predictions as they proceed through the story. For example, once they begin reading that the class is going to China, they will probably want to refine their predictions about the fortune cookie. After completing the book, give students an opportunity to confirm or reject their predictions, and discuss how much easier it is to predict what will happen in a book when they are "armed" with some knowledge.

During-reading Activity: This activity accomplishes several goals. It forces students to monitor their comprehension as they read, has them "actively reading" because they are thinking as they read, has students find details in the book, and sets a purpose for reading. The friendship between Amber and Justin is central to the book's plot. Tell students that the author shows this to the reader not only by stating it, but also by showing the characters' behaviors. As students read the book, have them document "evidence" of Justin and Amber's friendship such as Amber being "absolutely positively sure that" Justin has something planned when he is ticking at the beginning of the story. Discuss why this is "evidence" of their friendship (she knows him so well, and other friends would not have understood why he was making that noise). After finding several examples in the book, let students write short paragraphs to document similar evidence of different characters' close relationships.

Post-reading Activity: Remind students that Amber was going to read the classic *Charlotte's Web* by E. B. White (HarperTrophy, 1952) and do a diorama for her book report. Have students make dioramas for *Amber Brown Is Not a Crayon*. Instruct each student to choose a scene from the book, then recreate that scene in a shoe box. Encourage students to include the characters and settings from the scenes, and to display them in ways that depict the main plot or idea of the book. If students complete the project in class, supply them with crayons, markers, construction paper, fabric, tracing paper, etc. When students are finished, display the dioramas in chronological order around the classroom.

Plot Predictions

comprehension reproducible for
Amber Brown Is Not a Crayon

Name_____ Date_____

Use this page to write predictions about the objects you see. You will be writing predictions before seeing the book, before reading it, and as you read.

Object: _____
1st prediction: _____
_____

Prediction after previewing: _____
_____

Prediction as I read: _____
_____

My prediction was: correct   somewhat correct   incorrect

Object: _____
1st prediction: _____
_____

Prediction after previewing: _____
_____

Prediction as I read: _____
_____

My prediction was: correct   somewhat correct   incorrect

Object: _____
1st prediction: _____
_____

Prediction after previewing: _____
_____

Prediction as I read: _____
_____

My prediction was: correct   somewhat correct   incorrect

Because of Winn-Dixie

by Kate DiCamillo

(Candlewick Press, 2000)

A girl named Opal finds a dog she names Winn-Dixie. He helps Opal learn that loving something does not mean that you won't lose it. This hopeful story teaches that happiness and sorrow can be felt together.

Related books: *Shiloh* by Phyllis Reynolds Naylor (Dell, 1991); *Strider* by Beverly Cleary (William Morrow & Company, 1991)

Phonemic Awareness Activities
for *Because of Winn-Dixie*

Pre-reading Activity: Demonstrate that whether a syllable is open or closed determines the vowel phoneme in the syllable. Write *Because of Winn-Dixie* on the board. Have students divide the words into syllables using slashes (*Be/cause of Winn-Dix/ie*). Ask what sound the letter e makes in the syllable *be* (long). Then, ask what sound the letter i makes in the syllable *Winn* (short). Repeat for *Dix* and *ie*. Write *Opal*, *preacher*, and *dog* on the board. Have students find a pattern for vowel sounds in the syllables. Explain that when a syllable ends with a vowel phoneme (like O in *Opal*, *prea* in *preacher*, *be* in *because*), it is an open syllable and usually makes a long vowel sound. When a syllable ends with a consonant phoneme such as *winn*, *dog*, *pal* in *Opal*, etc., it is a closed syllable and makes a short vowel sound, unless it is r-controlled, as in *preacher*. Practice the rule with words from the book's back cover or a newspaper.

During-reading Activity: While reading chapter 2, note how the preacher says "Hmmm" and "Mmmmmmmm-hmmm." Have students make these sounds. Ask if they can "hear" the preacher. What might the author have written if the preacher said no? ("Uh-uh.") As a class, write other sounds people make during conversations. Pause in chapter 5 when Winn-Dixie "sings" in church ("aaaaaaarrooo, arrrrooooowwww," etc.). Have students reread Winn-Dixie's "words," stretching out each sound. Was that a good way to spell Winn-Dixie's "words?" Explain that these sounds help readers "hear" characters. Distribute the Spelling Sounds reproducible (page 19). Have pairs "read" the noises and sounds that are represented with the graphemes. Have each pair make two noises and decide how to write them phonemically. Have partners try to read each others' sound words correctly.

Post-reading Activity: Write *because* on the board. Identify its phonemes (/b/, long /e/, /k/, short /o/, /z/). Ask what graphemes represent the short /o/ sound in the word (au). Explain that au is a vowel diphthong because together the letters make a special vowel phoneme. List the *au*, *aw*, *ou*, and *ow* digraphs on the board. Point out the similarities and differences in the phoneme pairs au/aw and ou/ow. Pass out word cards with words such as *law*, *fraud*, *cow*, *out*, etc. Have students read their word cards and walk around to find other students who have cards with the same vowel diphthong. All students who have au and aw words will form a group, and those with ou and ow will form another group. Then, review the groups' word cards to confirm or correct responses.

Spelling Sounds

phonemic awareness reproducible for
Because of Winn-Dixie

Names _____ Date _____

With your partner, say all of the sounds below. Think about what these sounds might represent. Then, make up and write two sounds together, and write how you think they are spelled on the blanks. Draw a picture of how one of these sounds is made.

1. Arrrroooooooo

2. Yoo-hoo

3. Awwwww

4. Woooooowee

5. Wah-wah-wah-waaaaah

6. _____

7. _____

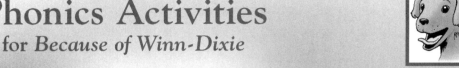

Phonics Activities
for *Because of Winn-Dixie*

Pre-reading Activity: Show the title to students and have them identify the final sound in *Dixie*. Ask students if the long /e/ sound is often represented by the letters ie. Challenge students to discover what graphemes usually represent the long /e/ sound by searching through newspaper or magazine articles and highlighting all of the long /e/ sounds. (They may also copy words from *Because of Winn-Dixie*.) Then, have students discover the usual pattern: final long /e/ is usually represented with the letter y, as in *happy*. Make a chart with two headers: one that is labeled *ie* and one labeled *y*. In these columns, write the words students found and discuss which column has more words.

During-reading Activity: While reading chapter 6, pause to discuss what Miss Franny thought Winn-Dixie was (a bear). Have students notice what letters make the /air/ sound in the word *bear* (ear). Ask students what the word *bear* would be if they removed the letter b (*ear*). Tell students that the vowel team ea with the letter r usually represents the /eer/ phoneme, like in *ear*. The letters ear also sometimes make the /er/ sound, like in *earth*, and the phoneme /air/ heard in *bear*. Rarely, the ear team also makes the /ar/ sound like in *heart*. Have students find other words while reading that contain the ear team and list them according to the different sounds they make. Some words to find in the book (after chapter 6) include *heart*, *appear*, *heard*, *hear*, *tear*, *fear*, and *swear*.

Post-reading Activity: Silent letters appear often, but none are more common than silent e. Point out that in *Because of Winn-Dixie*, *because* has a silent e. Copy the Silent E reproducible (page 21) and distribute it to students. Tell students to read the invitation Opal wrote for her party and highlight all occurrences of the silent e. Review all of the silent e words as a class. Then, have students write responses to the invitation and include as many silent e words as they can (they must make sense, though). Have students trade papers. Ask students to read their classmates' papers and circle all of the silent e words. Walk around the classroom during this part of the exercise to assess students' understanding of the concept. You may wish to award a prize for the most silent e words used correctly in a response. (Be sure to point out that the word *prize* also contains a silent e.)

Silent E
phonics reproducible for
Because of Winn-Dixie

Name_____ Date_____

Read the invitation below. Highlight each word that contains a silent e. Then, read the instructions below.

Dear Everyone,

I would like to invite you to a party! It will be kind of like the one Scarlett goes to in the book <u>Gone with the Wind</u>—except there will be egg-salad sandwiches instead of barbecue and there won't be so many people. Still, it will be great fun! The party will be held in Gloria Dump's backyard at night, so it will be cooler. There will be music, courtesy of Otis and his guitar. Sweetie Pie thought that a dog theme would be a great idea. We will also be serving Dump Punch, which is orange juice, grapefruit juice, and soda all mixed together. We will even have candles and Littmus Lozenges. Hope you'll come!

Sincerely,

Opal

Write a response on the lines below. Think about what party food or drink you might bring, when you might arrive, and questions you have. Or, you may decide that you cannot attend the party and need to explain why. Include as many silent e words as possible. Finally, trade papers with a friend and circle all of the silent e words in the response.

_____

_____

_____

_____

_____

_____

_____

_____

_____

_____

Vocabulary Activities
for *Because of Winn-Dixie*

Pre-reading Activity: Tell students that the story is about a girl named Opal and her father. Read the excerpt from chapter 2 where Opal explains why she calls her dad "the preacher" in her mind. Tell students that Opal's dad preaches, so he is called a preacher. Ask students, "What is the base word in *preacher, preaches,* and *preaching*? (preach)" Tell students that when you add letters to the ending of a word, it is called a *suffix.* Opal's dad is a preacher, or one who preaches. Ask students, "What is one who teaches called? (teacher)" Review the following suffixes and their meanings: ness (state of), less (without), ful (full of). Have students cut out the word and suffix cards on the Suffix Scramble reproducible (page 23). After reading each base word and suffix, have students put the cards together to form words with suffixes. See how many combinations they can make.

During-reading Activity: Although this book contains rich, descriptive language, the vocabulary is not very difficult or advanced. This activity will help students identify rich vocabulary and work with the words in and out of context. Give each student a strip of construction paper (about 5" x 9"). Instruct students to fold their papers vertically to make long, folded bookmarks. Allow each student to decorate the "cover" with the title, author's name, an illustration, and the words *Vocabulary Bookmark.* Tell students that they will be "collecting" words on their bookmarks that they find while reading. Explain the rule for word collecting is that each word must be new, confusing, interesting, or particularly descriptive. In order to help students understand what type of words they should be looking for, "collect" some words, such as *red-faced, concerned, hollered, trotting,* etc., as you read. Instruct each student to copy the sentence that the word is contained in, underline the word, then write a new sentence containing the word. Students will use their bookmarks throughout the reading of the book, so remind them to list only one or two words per chapter. Consider using these words for spelling tests and group activities, or have students compare lists.

Post-reading Activity: Review the definition of a noun. Remind students that a *proper noun* is capitalized because it is a noun that names a particular person, place, or thing. In the case of this book, the proper noun *Winn-Dixie* names not only a character but also a place. Any noun that does not name a particular person, place, or thing is a *common noun.* List common nouns from *Because of Winn-Dixie* on the board and have students look through the book to find a proper noun counterpart for each. Possible noun combinations are: dog (Winn-Dixie), man (Otis, Preacher), woman or lady (Miss Franny or Gloria Dump), girl (Opal, Sweetie Pie, or Amanda), boy (Dunlap, Stevie), parrot (Gertrude), book (*Gone with the Wind*), place (Winn-Dixie, Open Arms Baptist Church, Gertrude's Pet Store, Friendly Corners Trailer Park, Herman W. Block Memorial Library), librarian (Miss Franny), and candy (Littmus Lozenge).

Suffix Scramble
vocabulary reproducible for
Because of Winn-Dixie

Name_____ Date_____

Cut out the words cards and suffix cards. Mix and match the cards to make words. Write down all of the words you make.

ness	ful	er
less	kind	care
end	pain	hope
thank	color	dark
sing	paint	sad

Fluency Activities

for *Because of Winn-Dixie*

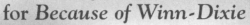

Pre-reading Activity: Discuss the importance of punctuation for fluent reading. Tell students that a comma can affect the way a sentence sounds and even what it means. Read the first sentence from *Because of Winn-Dixie* aloud with the correct punctuation. Then, read the same sentence without commas. Ask students what they notice about your reading without commas. (The answer will probably be that you ran out of breath!) Give students copies of the Pause, Please! reproducible (page 25). Instruct them to add necessary commas to each sentence. Then, have students take turns reading their sentences aloud. Note the differences in comma placements that change meanings.

During-reading Activity: Tell students that part of being a fluent reader is to read the text just as the author wrote it. Tell students that the author of this book wanted to make the characters seem realistic. One of the ways she did that was by writing the dialogue just the way the characters would sound in real life. It is important to read it just the way it is. For example, instead of writing "Winn-Dixie and I," the author writes "me and Winn-Dixie." Even though "Winn-Dixie and I" is correct, the other format is how the character would actually talk. Pause when encountering these scenes and take a few minutes to reread the section, giving students an opportunity to read them as well. For example, pause and read, "'You don't need a dog.' 'I know it,' I said. 'I know I don't need a dog.'" (*Because of Winn-Dixie*, page 17), and "Whooooeee. . . That takes the strange-name prize, don't it?" (*Because of Winn-Dixie*, page 65).

Post-reading Activity: Discuss how Opal reads *Gone with the Wind* to Gloria Dump. Ask students, "How do you think Opal sounded while she read? What makes a good oral reader? If you were listening to a story being read aloud, how would you want the reader to sound?" Discuss some of the characteristics of a fluent reader. Tell each student to select an excerpt from a book that he enjoyed and practice reading it aloud several times. Then, have each student choose one person to whom he will read aloud, like Opal did for Gloria. This "person" might be a younger sibling, an older relative, a parent, or even a stuffed animal. After completing the assignment, ask students to report on their experiences of reading aloud. Have them ask the people to whom they read what was best about the reading.

Name_____ Date_____

Read the sentences below. Insert commas where you think they should go. Then, read the sentences again. Remember to pause where you put commas.

I told the preacher to write down what we needed at the store and that was bread butter eggs tuna fish sticks milk bones for the dog and honey.

On the right wall tapestries are hung.

He said "Mary Anne are you all right?"

It was a sunny windy day and leaves blew off the trees into the street.

Things I won't eat include coconut cake chocolate pie and celery.

She saw the boy who entered the room and shuddered.

My brother Tom likes pancakes for dinner.

Lynnette my sister needs to mow the lawn.

Comprehension Activities
for *Because of Winn-Dixie*

Pre-reading Activity: Tell students that a dog, Winn-Dixie, changes the main character's life. Have students think of people (or animals) who have changed or affected their lives. Discuss an experience from your life. Tell students that in the book, Opal creates lists to describe her mother and her dog. Have each student complete a copy of the Ten Things I Like about You reproducible (page 27) by writing a list of ten things she likes or admires about someone special. Then, have students draw pictures of themselves with their special people. Display the pictures on a bulletin board. After completing the book, discuss how Opal realizes "that a list of things couldn't even begin to show somebody the real Winn-Dixie, just like a list of ten things couldn't ever get me to know my mama." (*Because of Winn-Dixie*, page 164). Revisit students' lists and discuss whether they truly "capture" or describe the people they wrote about.

During-reading Activity: Tell students that the author uses *anthropomorphism* throughout her book to make Winn-Dixie seem almost like a person. Anthropomorphism is the attribution of human feelings, qualities, and/or motives to an animal, object, or idea. Have each student write this definition at the top of a sheet of paper and keep the sheet handy throughout the reading. As students read the book, have them jot down examples of anthropomorphism in the book (places in the text where Winn-Dixie does something like a human). Discuss how this affects the story line, the reader's connection to the story, and the reader's emotions. To extend the activity, let students write short paragraphs about their pets or objects by describing things that make them seem human as well.

Post-reading Activity: Review cause and effect, if necessary. After completing the book, have students refer back to the title. Ask them, "Why do you think the author chose this title? Do you think it's a good title? Why or why not? What does the title mean?" Discuss with students how everything that happens in the story is somehow "because of Winn-Dixie." In other words, Winn-Dixie is the cause of many effects in the book. Have students go through the story and make lists of things that happened "because of Winn-Dixie."

Ten Things I Like about You

comprehension reproducible for
Because of Winn-Dixie

Name_____ Date_____

Think of someone who has changed your life for the better. On the lines below, write ten characteristics about that person.

1. _____

2. _____

3. _____

4. _____

5. _____

6. _____

7. _____

8. _____

9. _____

10. _____

(Random House, 1987)

Gregory is a talented boy who moves to a new neighborhood. His Uncle Max is sharing his room, and a boy at his new school teases him. Gregory finds solace in a burned-out building by drawing a chalk garden on the black walls. Soon, this magical "garden" changes everything for him.

Related books: *The Paintbrush Kid* by Clyde Robert Bulla (Random House, 1998); *Shoeshine Girl* by Clyde Robert Bulla (HarperCollins, 1989)

Phonemic Awareness Activities
for *The Chalk Box Kid*

Pre-reading Activity: Review long and short /a/. Have students give examples of words for each sound. List them on the board under the headings *Long /a/* and *Short /a/*. Ask, "Can the letter a represent any other phonemes?" Record the guesses. Then, read the book title. Ask students which word contains a phoneme represented by the letter a (*chalk*). Ask under which heading the word belongs. When students discover that the /a/ in *chalk* is not long or short, have them repeat the sound a makes in *chalk* (short /o/ sound, as in *ox*, although it is l-controlled). Distribute the Sounds of A reproducible (page 29). Once word cards are sorted, explain that a often makes the short /o/ sound when preceded by w as in *water*, followed by the letter l as in *ball*, or is part of vowel digraphs au or aw as in *fraud* and *saw*.

During-reading Activity: As you read chapter 2, ask the following questions and record the answers on the board: "Why was Uncle Max coming?" (He was staying with them.) "What did Gregory do when he found out Uncle Max was coming?" (He explored the neighborhood.) "What did Uncle Max call Gregory?" (The Paintbrush Kid.) "What did Gregory do to show his anger?" (He kicked the gate.) Have students reread the answers. Ask them what the words *staying, paintbrush, neighborhood,* and *gate* have in common (the long /a/ sound). Have a student come to the board and underline the letters in each word that make the long /a/ sound. Point out how the long /a/ sound is represented by different graphemes in each word: ay, ai, ei, and a_e. As students read, have them list words that have the long /a/ sound. Use the words *staying, paint, neighborhood,* and *gate* as headers. Have students compare lists as they read more chapters.

Post-reading Activity: Write *garden* on the board. Ask what phonemes students hear in the first syllable (/g/, /ar/). Explain that when a vowel is followed by an r, it is called an *r-controlled vowel*. This is because the r "controls" the vowel sound, and does not make the true /r/ sound, as in *rain*. Write *dirt, verb,* and *turn* on the board. Point out that the vowel and r make the same phoneme in all of the words. Have pairs list words found in the book that have r-controlled vowels and underline the vowels and r's that make the r-controlled sound.

Name_____ Date_____

Read the words below. If the letter a makes the long a sound as in *gate*, highlight the word with yellow. If the letter a makes the short a sound as in *happy*, highlight the word with orange. If the letter a makes the short o sound as in *chalk*, highlight the word with pink. After you have highlighted all of the words, cut them out and sort them according to their sounds. Then, try to figure out the pattern for the short /o/ words.

hat	walk	change
crawl	false	at
talk	watch	call
want	say	apple
take	bawl	ball

Phonics Activities
for *The Chalk Box Kid*

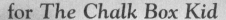re-reading Activity: List the following character names on the board: *Gregory, Ivy, Miss Perry.* Explain that these are the names of some of the characters in *The Chalk Box Kid.* Ask students if they notice anything in common between the three names. (They all end in y.) Ask students what sound the y makes at the end of the names (long /e/). Remind students that the letter y is sometimes a consonant and sometimes a vowel. When it is used as a consonant, it makes the /y/ sound, as in *yell.* When it is used as a vowel, it makes the long /e/ sound, the long /i/ sound, or occasionally the short /i/ sound as in *gypsy.* Give students magazines or newspaper articles, and have them highlight all of the words that contain the letter y. Challenge students to find the phonetic patterns for the letter y as a consonant and as a vowel. Guide students to discover that the letter y represents its consonant sound when it begins a word or syllable; otherwise, it represents a vowel sound.

uring-reading Activity: Write the title on the board and have students repeat it. Underline the word *box.* Ask students what letters represent the phoneme for x (/ks/). This is a difficult phoneme so students may need some prompting. Explain that /ks/ is always the sound the letter x makes, unless it is at the beginning of a word. Have students help you list other words in the ox word family such as *fox, pox,* and *ox.* Then, give each student an X Marks the Spot reproducible (page 31). Have students fill in examples of other words that contain the letter x.

ost-reading Activity: Using children's literature to assess phonics skills in older students is a good strategy because the reading will be grade level even if the skills practice students need is remedial. Use a paragraph of *The Chalk Box Kid* for assessment in phonics and spelling. Choose a paragraph that contains words which include phonics skills you want to assess, such as a particular word family, silent e, initial blends, etc. Instruct each student to take out a sheet of paper and a pencil, and be prepared to take dictation. Read the paragraph to them slowly and have them write the paragraph exactly as you read it. Collect papers and compare them to the original. Use the results to determine which lessons students need to relearn. After reteaching, consider repeating the dictation activity to reassess.

X Marks the Spot

phonics reproducible for
The Chalk Box Kid

Name_____ Date_____

Under each vowel and letter x, list as many words as you can think of which contain those letters. Use a dictionary to think of more complicated words. One row in each category is filled in for you.

ax
taxes

_____

_____

_____

_____

_____

_____

_____

ex
exact

_____

_____

_____

_____

_____

_____

_____

ix
mixture

_____

_____

_____

_____

_____

_____

_____

_____

ox
toxic

_____

_____

_____

_____

_____

_____

_____

_____

ux
luxury

_____

_____

_____

_____

_____

Vocabulary Activities
for *The Chalk Box Kid*

Pre-reading Activity: Help students understand vocabulary as well as preview the text. Prior to reading each chapter, have students skim it. Instruct each student to list each unknown word, the page on which it is found, and the sentence in which it is used. Have students write the total number of unknown words at the tops of their papers when they have finished skimming the chapter. Then, divide students into groups and have them share their unknown words. Students should help each other decide what each word means by using either prior knowledge or the context of the sentence in which the word was found. After the groups have met, have each student count to see if his total number of unknown words has remained the same or if it has been reduced through classmates' help.

During-reading Activity: This activity is not only an excellent way to teach vocabulary, it also provides students with an opportunity to practice critical thinking. Distribute one reproducible to each student, and assign each student a chapter. (You may also want to let students have seven copies of the reproducible and work with all of the vocabulary words.) Assign the following vocabulary words: chapter 1—*bare*; chapter 2—*important*; chapter 3—*brag*; chapter 4—*plink*; chapter 5—*grand*; chapter 6—*nursery*; chapter 7—*rubbed*; chapter 8—*pretending*; chapter 9—*puzzled*. As students encounter each word, have them use the New Word Analysis reproducible (page 33) to analyze and define the word. Each student should fill in the blanks with the chapter and page number, the word, the sentence in which the word can be found, her guess of the word's meaning, the actual dictionary definition, the sentence from the book with a synonym in place of the original word, and why she thinks this word "represents" or is important for this chapter. For example, the word *bare* is important for, or representative of, chapter 1 because the main idea of this chapter is that when Gregory moves into a new home, his room is bare, but he is excited and makes it his own. Finally, have students illustrate an example of each word. For words that are harder to illustrate, help students by making suggestions. For example, for *important*, each student could draw something that is important to her. Let each student fill out a reproducible for each word, or assign the words to small groups.

Post-reading Activity: Tell students that the characters are very important to the development and "feel" of this book. List the characters on the board and ask students to skim through the book to find events, dialogue, etc. that help the reader decide what "kind" of person each character is. For example, discuss how Uncle Max covered Gregory's drawings with his own posters without asking. Then, ask students to think of an adjective that would describe Uncle Max such as *rude, impolite, selfish,* etc. Once students understand the assignment, assign groups and give each group a thesaurus. Challenge each group to come up with the most adjectives to describe each character. After an allotted amount of time, have groups take turns sharing their adjectives for each character. Compare responses and correct any words that are not adjectives. Allow groups to create character posters that list the adjectives. Display the posters in the classroom.

New Word Analysis
vocabulary reproducible for
The Chalk Box Kid

Name_____ Date_____

Read the directions and complete the tasks to help you understand a new word.

1. Chapter:_____ Page word is found on: _____ Word:_____

2. Sentence containing the word: _____
_____
_____

3. What I think the word means: _____
_____

4. Dictionary definition: _____
_____
_____

5. Rewrite the sentence using a synonym for the vocabulary word. _____
_____
_____

6. Why do you think this word is important for this chapter? _____
_____
_____

7. Illustrate the word below.

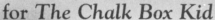

Pre-reading Activity: Tell students that the main character, Gregory, gets teased in this book. Ask students to share experiences they might have had with being teased and how the "teasers" sounded when they spoke. Give each student a copy of the Don't Tease Me! reproducible (page 35), or make a transparency for an overhead projector and read the passage aloud once to students. Have students notice your tone of voice as you read the dialogue. Then, ask students to volunteer to be different characters, and take turns rereading the passage. Encourage the class to comment on how each student sounds—very expressive, angry, sad, etc. Tell students that it is important to read dialogue in an expressive manner, even "in their heads." Explain that this is part of being a fluent reader, which helps readers understand and "feel" what a character is thinking. This is especially important in a book such as *The Chalk Box Kid* which has emotion and dialogue.

During-reading Activity: The author uses italicized words throughout the book. When you encounter one, pause and ask students what they notice about that sentence. Tell students that when an author uses "slanted letters" it is called *italics*, and the reader must stress, or emphasize, the italicized word. Reread the sentence aloud, stressing the italicized word, and ask students why they think the author chose this word to italicize. Then, have students practice reading the sentence aloud while stressing the word. As you proceed through the book, have students watch for other italicized words. When they find one, stop to discuss why it is italicized and how the sentence should be read.

Post-reading Activity: Assign students to pairs or small groups. Have each group select an excerpt from the book to "present" orally to the class. Tell students that they should look for an excerpt with a lot of dialogue and emotion such as when Uncle Max arrives and Gregory is unhappy, or when Vance is teasing Gregory. Give students time to select their excerpts, assign parts, and practice reading them orally. Remind students that although they should not memorize their parts, they must be comfortable enough with the text to not stumble on the words. Students must also be expressive, so encourage them to think about how the characters must sound when they are talking (angry, teasing, sad, etc.). Then, have groups read their parts in front of the class. After each group presents, ask group members what made them choose that excerpt.

Don't Tease Me!

fluency reproducible for
The Chalk Box Kid

Name_____ Date_____

Listen to your teacher read the dialogue. Then, choose a character and read the passage aloud with a partner. Draw a picture of the scene below.

Gregory was the new kid in school. He hoped he'd make friends, but it already looked like that might not happen. It was the first day, and one boy was already being mean to him. Vance was the biggest kid in school.

"Hey, how come you said your old school is so big?" Vance asked.

"I didn't say it was so big, I just said it was big. It just seemed that way to me, that's all." Gregory didn't understand what was the big deal.

"You think your old school was better than this one? Do ya', huh?" Vance teased. Now there were other kids listening. "You like to brag, huh? You're a bragger!"

"I am not! I am not bragging. I just said it was big."

Comprehension Activities
for *The Chalk Box Kid*

Pre-reading Activity: Explain that Gregory, the main character, is very artistic. His talent is drawing. Ask students to think of their talents. Have students respond in writing to the following prompt: I am talented at _____. Encourage students to include details. Then, go around the room and let students share talents. If possible, let some students demonstrate.

During-reading Activity: Tell students that some books do not have titles for each chapter, but this book does. Explain that a chapter title gives you a clue as to what will happen in the chapter, just like the title of a story does. Before reading each chapter, read the chapter title and have students use it to guess what will happen in the chapter. After reading the chapter, revisit the chapter title and have students decide if that title was a good choice for the chapter. Finally, have students think of other good titles for that chapter. Remind students that the main idea of the chapter should be kept in mind when writing chapter titles. Use the What's in a Chapter Name? reproducible (page 37) to help students complete the activity. (Each student will need three copies of the reproducible, unless you want to limit the activity to three chapters per student.)

Post-reading Activity: Tell students that when they read, they should be seeing everything in their "Brain TVs." Explain that "Brain TVs" are like screens in their imaginations in which they should see and hear all of the action, just like on a television screen in real life. This reading strategy is called *visualizing.* Tell each student to skim through the book and pick one scene that he can really "see" in his head. Give each student a sheet of black construction paper and a piece of chalk. Tell students to draw their scenes on their papers using chalk, and to bring the scenes "to life," just like Gregory did with his garden. Have students discuss why they chose these particular scenes, and help them list words that made the scenes visual. Display the drawings on a bulletin board titled "The Chalk Box Kids."

What's in a Chapter Name?
comprehension reproducible for
The Chalk Box Kid

Name_____ Date_____

In the blanks below, write the number and name of each chapter, your predictions about what will happen, your evaluation of the author's title choices, and your choices for new chapter titles.

Chapter __ title: _____

Based on the chapter title, I predict that this chapter will be about: _____
_____

Now that I have read the chapter, I think this was a _____ choice for a title because
_____

Another good title for this chapter would be: _____

Chapter __ title: _____

Based on the chapter title, I predict that this chapter will be about: _____
_____

Now that I have read the chapter, I think this was a _____ choice for a title because
_____

Another good title for this chapter would be: _____

Chapter __ title: _____

Based on the chapter title, I predict that this chapter will be about: _____
_____

Now that I have read the chapter, I think this was a _____ choice for a title because
_____

Another good title for this chapter would be: _____

Charlotte's Web

(HarperTrophy, 1952)

by E. B. White

Students will love the touching story of Wilbur, a pig who is saved from slaughter by Charlotte, a spider. Charlotte makes Wilbur famous by spelling things like "some pig" on her web. The theme of friendship, unique characters, rich language, and well-developed plot captivate readers.

Related books: *James and the Giant Peach* by Roald Dahl (Alfred A. Knopf, 1961); *Stuart Little* by E. B. White (HarperCollins, 1974); *Trumpet of the Swan* by E. B. White (HarperTrophy, 1973)

Phonemic Awareness Activities
for *Charlotte's Web*

Pre-reading Activity: Without letting students see the cover, read the title aloud. Ask what sound is at the beginning of *Charlotte's* (/sh/) and what letters usually represent the /sh/ sound. Show the title and point out that *Charlotte* begins with the digraph ch. Explain that the consonant digraph *ch* usually makes the /ch/ sound, like in *chat*. Sometimes ch makes the /k/ sound, like in *school*. Very rarely, the ch makes the /sh/ sound like in *Charlotte*. Pair students and give each partner one of the two word lists on the Ch Digraph reproducible (page 39). Have students call out the words on their lists. Their partners must identify which phoneme they hear: /sh/, /ch/, or /k/. Use this in conjunction with the phonics pre-reading activity.

During-reading Activity: Pause while reading the scene in chapter 12 when Charlotte asks how to spell *terrific*. Reread the goose's answer. Have students note how the goose "said" the letter c as "see" and the letter i as "eye." Point out how the name of the letter c is actually pronounced the same way as the word *see* and how the name of the letter i is pronounced the same way as the word *eye*. Now, ask students to go back to the beginning of the chapter and notice how the goslings responded when called at the meeting: "Bee-bee-bee!" (*Charlotte's Web*, page 86). Ask students what letter name sounds the same as this word (b). Ask students if they can think of how to spell other letter names, such as d/dee, f/ef, g/jee, j/jay, k/kay, etc. (Some of these will be real words, too.)

Post-reading Activity: Work with rhymes creatively by having each student write a rhyming poem about a character. Have each student choose a character. Then, choose one of your own and demonstrate how to go through the alphabet searching for words that rhyme with the character name's word ending. For example, if you choose Wilbur, as you go through the alphabet you will find the rhymes *blur, cur, fur, her, over, per, sir, under,* and *were*. Provide assistance as students are writing. Post the poems on a bulletin board titled "Some Poems!"

Name_____ Date_____

Read your list of ch words aloud to your partner. Have your partner tell you whether he or she hears the sh, ch, or k phoneme.

Partner 1	Partner 2
Michigan	schedule
chemical	chocolate
character	Chicago
stomach	chilly
chore	technical
couch	children
reach	peach
orchard	machine
Charlotte	chorus
chariot	orchestra
echo	ache
each	channel
teach	chemistry
chair	ouch

Phonics Activities

for *Charlotte's Web*

Pre-reading Activity: This activity correlates to the phonemic awareness pre-reading activity. Read the title to students and ask them what sound the ch digraph makes at the beginning of the word *Charlotte's* (/sh/). After reviewing the sounds the ch digraph makes, ask students what other digraph makes the /sh/ sound (sh). Tell students that although the ch digraph can make the /ch/, /k/, and /sh/ sounds, the sh digraph consistently makes the /sh/ sound. Have students complete the Digraph Challenge reproducible (page 41) to reinforce this concept.

During-reading Activity: Discuss how Charlotte spells things on her web to try to save Wilbur. This activity can be set up as a center, where students can go to spell different words they encounter as they read, or can be done as a whole-class activity. Give each student a piece of black construction paper and a length of white yarn. Tell students that they will be spelling words by using the yarn to connect letters like Charlotte did on her web. (The black construction paper will serve as a background so the "webbing" will stand out.) If you would like each student to "write" in cursive, she can leave the yarn in one long piece. If you'd prefer they print, have them cut the yarn into smaller pieces. The words can vary according to your needs and objectives; students can spell vocabulary from the story, characters' names, words that Charlotte writes, or words that contain certain phonics patterns (such as long /a/ words, words beginning with the ch digraph, etc.). This can also be used for a quick assessment because you can walk around the room and scan students' knowledge of specific phonics skills.

Post-reading Activity: Use the animals in the book to make this word family activity more sophisticated for third graders. Write the words *pig*, *rat*, *goose*, and *sheep* on the board and have each student list them as column headers at the top of a sheet of paper. Tell students that you will give them two minutes to write as many word family words as possible under each header. Time students as they write. Then, have each student read out his word family words. Give a small story-related prize, such as an animal bookmark or a pig-shaped eraser, to the student with the most correct words under each column.

 First-Rate Reading™ Grade 3 • CD-0071 • © Carson-Dellosa

Digraph Challenge
phonics reproducible for
Charlotte's Web

Name_____   Date_____

You know that the consonant digraph sh makes the sh sound, like in *sheep*. The consonant digraph ch makes the ch sound like in *church*, and the k sound like in *mechanic*, but it also makes the sh sound like in *Charlotte*.

Brainstorm words that contain the sh and ch digraphs. Then, list them under the correct column below. Underline or highlight the digraphs. If you run out of ideas, search in the book *Charlotte's Web*, newspaper articles, or magazines.

sh	ch		
	(k)	(sh)	(ch)
_____	_____	_____	_____
_____	_____	_____	_____
_____	_____	_____	_____
_____	_____	_____	_____
_____	_____	_____	_____
_____	_____	_____	_____

Vocabulary Activities
for *Charlotte's Web*

re-reading Activity: Because the story's setting is critical to the plot, it is important that students are familiar with the concept of a farm and many of its related vocabulary words. It is also important that students understand what a runt is, since characters' reactions to that word begin the entire story. Ask students to share any experiences they have had on farms and any knowledge they have about farms. Have students brainstorm words that have to do with farms such as things they might see, smell, hear, etc. Create a web with the word *farm* in the middle and list student responses around the web. Consider "implanting" some ideas, words, or concepts that you know will arise in the book such as what kinds of jobs people have on a farm, what kinds of animals are on a farm, etc. Then, introduce the word *runt*. Ask students if they know what a runt is. Tell students that this is the story of a pig who was born a runt—the smallest and weakest of the litter. Have students predict what might happen to an animal who is born as the runt of a litter.

During-reading Activity: Throughout the book, Charlotte uses words that are new to Wilbur. When Wilbur asks what they mean, Charlotte always tells him. Have students create *Charlotte's Web* Dictionaries by recording all of the new words they (and Wilbur) learn from Charlotte. Each time students come to a part when Charlotte explains what a word means, instruct each student to write the word on the Charlotte's Wonderful Words reproducible (page 43), write the definition according to Charlotte, and then use it in a sentence. Students may need more than one reproducible as they learn new words. Have students punch holes in the pages and use loose-leaf paper rings, chenille craft sticks, or yarn to bind the pages together. Then, let students design covers for their dictionaries.

Post-reading Activity: Discuss Charlotte's choices of words used to describe Wilbur. Ask students if they felt that the words were good descriptors for Wilbur and have them list other words Charlotte might have used in her webs. Review the concept of adjectives. Have students make their own webs to describe people in the same positive way that Charlotte describes Wilbur. Students can describe themselves, classmates, or characters from the book. Encourage each student to make a preliminary list of possible adjectives and then select the one or two she thinks are most accurate. Give each student a sheet of black construction paper. Show students how to draw webs with white crayons. Then, have each student trace her describing word or phrase on her web with silver glitter to look like the morning dew reflecting on Charlotte's web. Display projects on a bulletin board titled "Sparkly, Shiny Adjective Webs."

Charlotte's Wonderful Words
vocabulary reproducible for
Charlotte's Web

Name_____ Date_____

Each time you read a new word that is used by Charlotte, write it in one of the blanks below. Next to the word, write Charlotte's definition. Then, write a sentence that contains the word.

Word: _____   Definition: _____

_____

Sentence: _____

_____

Word: _____   Definition: _____

_____

Sentence: _____

_____

Word: _____   Definition: _____

_____

Sentence: _____

_____

Word: _____   Definition: _____

_____

Sentence: _____

_____

_____

re-reading Activity: Tell students that the book begins with an argument between Fern and her father. Mr. Arable wants to kill the runt pig of the litter, while Fern thinks this is a terrible injustice. Have each student think of a time he has argued with a parent or guardian. Discuss what the conversations were like. Were their voices soft or loud? Did they speak slowly and calmly, or urgently and anxiously? Have students pair up to write skits about children arguing with their parents. One student in each group will play a child, and the other will play a parent. Have students practice reading their skits aloud, focusing on making the skit sound realistic. Then, let pairs present their skits to the class. Discuss whether they read fluently and whether the arguments were believable. Direct students to keep this in mind when they read the opening pages of *Charlotte's Web*.

uring-reading Activity: Students' oral reading is often better when they are reading something they wrote themselves. Have students practice their fluency by writing and reading announcements about different events from the story. After reading chapter 1, have each student write a birth announcement for Wilbur. After reading chapter 20, have each student write a newspaper announcement for Wilbur's prize. Finally, after Charlotte's babies are born, have each student write another birth announcement. Give students an opportunity to practice reading their announcements aloud several times. Once students feel they are fluent, have them take turns reading their announcements to the class, a small group, or a partner. Use the Extra! Extra! Read All about It! reproducible (page 45) for each fluency writing assignment.

ost-reading Activity: This is a particularly good book to use for readers' theater because the characters have such distinct personalities and speech styles. Assign students to groups. Have each group select a scene to act out. Have students choose character parts (and narrators). Give students paper plates, construction paper, etc., to make character masks. Make sure that students can still read and speak easily while wearing the masks. Have students practice reading their scenes several times. Remind students to use expressive voices, try to sound like the characters, pause appropriately, use voice intonations, and read smoothly and naturally. Have groups present their skits to the class. If a video camera is available, tape the scenes in order, then watch the tape as a class.

Extra! Extra! Read All about It!

fluency reproducible for
Charlotte's Web

Name_____ Date_____

On the lines below, write a headline for your announcement. In the headline, use words that will capture the listeners' interest. Then, use the book to write information about the event. What happened? What characters were present? Add any interesting details that help explain the event and why it is important enough for an announcement.

_____

(headline)

_____

_____

_____

_____

_____

_____

_____

_____

Comprehension Activities
for *Charlotte's Web*

Pre-reading Activity: Tell students that *Charlotte's Web* is a book about friendship. Have students think about what friendship is, what kinds of things friends do for each other, what it means to be a true friend, etc. Then, have them write journal-type entries about friendship. Encourage students to use "stream of consciousness" writing where they "just write" what comes to mind on the topic. Have students pair up to share their responses and discuss friendship with each other. Consider repeating this activity after reading the book and compare those essays to the first ones.

During-reading Activity: Because of the emotional topics in this book, it is a great story to use with dialogue journals. A dialogue journal is similar to a reader's response journal in that, throughout the reading, the student writes her thoughts/reactions/responses to each chapter. The difference, however, is that with a dialogue journal, students exchange journals and write to each other as well. Give each student two sheets of construction paper for journal covers. Have students decorate covers with the book title, author, illustrations, their names, and the heading "Dialogue Journal." Have them staple the covers around several sheets of notebook paper to create journals. As students finish reading each chapter, have them respond in their journals. Students can write about what they thought, felt, were confused about, etc. However, students must finish each entry with a question for their journal partners such as *What do you think will happen next?* or *Do you think it's a good idea for Charlotte to write these webs for Wilbur?* Then, assign partners, but make sure that students who have already read the entire book swap with other students who have read it so that nothing is given away. When each student exchanges journals with a partner, the partner can read the journal entry and respond to the question. Encourage students not to worry too much about "rules," but to correspond naturally. Consider modeling a few entries of your own at the beginning and exchanging with student responses.

Post-reading Activity: A Somebody-Wanted-But-So Then (SWBST) chart is a popular and effective graphic organizer used to summarize literature. For example, *Somebody* (Wilbur) *wanted* to live *but* the Zuckermans were going to kill him and eat him, *so then* Charlotte wrote words in her webs to make him famous. In *Charlotte's Web*, the responses will differ greatly depending on which character is used. If the chart is focused on Templeton, for example, the responses would be very different because Templeton just wants to eat! By completing the SWBST Chart (page 47) about different characters, students not only summarize the story, but view it from the different characters' perspectives. They will also be able to see the interrelationships between the characters. Additionally, you can use the reproducible to prompt a discussion about how a character's desires change at different points in the story. For example, at the beginning Wilbur wanted to save himself, but at the end Wilbur wanted to save Charlotte's babies. You may wish to have students work on different scenes for one character as a class, or assign a different character to each student.

SWBST Chart
comprehension reproducible for
Charlotte's Web

Name_____ Date_____

Complete the Somebody-Wanted-But-So Then chart below.

Somebody: _____

Wanted: _____

_____

_____

_____

But: _____

_____

_____

_____

So then: _____

_____

_____

_____

Freckle Juice
by Judy Blume

(Simon and Schuster Books for Young Children, 1971)

Andrew wanted freckles like Nicky's. When Andrew asks Nicky how he got his freckles, his classmate Sharon offers to sell Andrew her "secret freckle recipe." Andrew tries freckle juice, but it doesn't work out quite as planned. Excellent for less proficient readers, this book is simple, funny, and relatively short.

Related books: *How to Eat Fried Worms* by Thomas Rockwell (Yearling, 1953); *The One in the Middle is the Green Kangaroo* by Judy Blume (Atheneum, 2000); *Tales of a Fourth Grade Nothing* by Judy Blume (Yearling, 1976)

Phonemic Awareness Activities
for *Freckle Juice*

Pre-reading Activity: Have students name the consonant blend at the beginning of freckle (/fr/). When two consonants are put together, but each letter still makes its own sound, it is called a *blend*. Ask if they can think of another consonant that makes a blend with the letter f (l). Have students repeat the blends as you point out differences in tongue placement. Say a list of /fl/ and /fr/ words, such as *fraction, frost, fry, fruit, flag, flake, fly,* and *flour*. Let students indicate if each word is a /fl/ blend or a /fr/ blend by forming uppercase l's or lowercase r's with their hands. Encourage students to listen for other words that contain /fr/ and /fl/ while reading *Freckle Juice*.

During-reading Activity: After reading chapter 1, discuss Sharon's offer to sell Andrew her secret recipe. How much did Sharon say the recipe would cost? (fifty cents). Write *cents* on the board. Ask students to indicate what two letters make the /s/ sound. Review that the letter c also makes the /k/ sound. Ask students to name examples of each. Divide the class into two teams and line them up on opposite sides of the room. Give the first student in each line a rock and a sponge to hold behind his back. Hold up an object or flash a word/picture card that contains either the hard or soft c sound. The two competing students must determine if the letter c is making a hard or soft sound, and should hold up either the rock or sponge to answer. The first player who correctly identifies the sound gets a point, then each student passes the rock and sponge to the next student in line and goes to the back. Then, the next two students compete. The game continues until all cards are used or every student has had a turn. The team with the most points wins.

Post-reading Activity: Write *Judy, Blume, Andrew,* and *juice* on the board. Have students read the words silently and find the common phoneme (/oo/). Say the long /u/ sound and the /oo/ sound to show the difference (long /u/ like in fuel). Explain that the /oo/ sound is represented by different graphemes (u, ue, ew, and ui). Write *tune, new,* and *due* on the board. Ask students to identify which graphemes make the /oo/ sound in these words. Have students cut out the Oo or U word cards (page 49), shuffle them, read them aloud, and sort them into long /u/ and /oo/ piles. (Note that some phonics programs consider both of these sounds to be long /u/.)

Oo or U

phonemic awareness reproducible for
Freckle Juice

Name_____ Date_____

Cut out the cards and shuffle them. Look at the word on each card. Say it aloud. Sort it into either the /oo/ or long /u/ category. If you work with a partner, you and your partner may pronounce some of these words differently.

few	fume	cruise
true	fruit	suit
glue	argue	due
human	value	chew
attitude	tune	flute

Phonics Activities
for *Freckle Juice*

Pre-reading Activity: Tell students that in the book, the main character buys a recipe for freckle juice. Discuss what a recipe is and whether there is such a thing as a secret recipe for something such as freckles. Give each student a copy of the Hiccups for Phonics reproducible (page 51). Have students highlight one or more of the phonetic patterns you have covered in class. Some possible phonetic patterns to identify include hard and soft c, hard and soft g, words with added endings (ly, s), words with silent letters, long and short vowels, etc.

During-reading Activity: This activity correlates to the phonemic awareness during-reading activity. Once students can identify the phonemes /k/ and /s/ for hard and soft c, have them find the phonetic pattern for the rule. If you do not have a class set of *Freckle Juice*, provide a few copies at a center. As students read the book, have them list all of the words that contain the letter c on separate sheets of paper. Direct students to try to find a pattern in the hard/soft c words as their lists become longer. Some words they might encounter in the first chapter of the book are *Marcus, covered, face, class, once, count, called, cents, secret, juice*, etc. Guide students to discover the rule: the letter c makes the hard c (/k/) sound except when followed by e, i, or y.

Post-reading Activity: Ask students to recall what happened after Andrew drank the freckle juice. (He got a stomachache.) Write the word *stomachache* on the board. Ask students what sound the letters ch make in this word /k/. Ask students what other sound the letters ch can make (/ch/ as in *change*). Tell students that the ch digraph almost always makes the /ch/ sound, but sometimes it makes the /k/ sound, and it rarely makes the /sh/ sound as in machine. Challenge students to try to prove this statement by skimming the book and listing the ch words according to their sounds: /ch/, /k/, and /sh/. Set a time limit for this activity. After sharing the ch words from the book, have students cut out ch words from a newspaper or magazine at home, then bring them to class in envelopes. Create a bar graph on a bulletin board to show how often the ch digraph makes each sound. Paste each word under its correct sound. You may also allow each student to create an individual bar graph, then compare graphs to see if everyone found about the same ratio of ch words for each sound.

Hiccups for Phonics

phonics reproducible for
Freckle Juice

Name_____ Date_____

Read the recipe below. Circle the following phonics patterns: _____

_____

_____

_____

Secret Recipe for Getting Rid of Hiccups

Serving size:

1 glass

Ingredients:

One cup of grape juice

Two tablespoons of sugar

A speck of cinnamon

Four drops of lemon juice

One ounce of powdered ginger

One teaspoon of salt

Three ice cubes

Directions:

Mix all of the ingredients in a glass.

Stir gently. Hold your nose and drink really fast.

Hiccups should be gone immediately.

Vocabulary Activities
for *Freckle Juice*

Pre-reading Activity: Because the concept of freckles is so critical to the story's plot, it is important that students understand this vocabulary word. This simple and fun activity will do the trick! Read the title to students and tell them that the main character wants freckles. Write the word on the board and ask students what freckles are. Have any students who have freckles stand up and show them to the class. Ask students how a person gets freckles. Tell students that in the book, Andrew buys a "secret recipe" for freckles. Ask students if they think this is possible. Tell them that they are about to "magically" get freckles. Then, draw freckles on students' cheeks with a brown or black makeup pencil. Take pictures with an instant or digital camera and post them on a bulletin board or Web page titled "We Drank *Freckle Juice!*"

During-reading Activity: Give each student a copy of the New Word Swap reproducible (page 53). In the first column, tell her to list 10 new or confusing words she encounters while reading. In the second column, have her copy the sentences from the text that contain the words and the page number on which she found them. Then, collect the papers and randomly redistribute them. On their classmates' papers, in the third column, have each student choose one new or confusing word and write a different word that would make sense in place of the unfamiliar word. Continue swapping papers until all words have been substituted. Return papers to their owners, then discuss and check students' word sheets to confirm or correct vocabulary understanding.

Post-reading Activity: Provide sample recipes for students to read. Talk about the common elements of recipes such as servings, measurements, ingredient names, cooking and mixing directions, etc. Have students look for these elements in the story recipe. Then, have them write recipes using vocabulary words from the story. These words can be taken from the student lists created in the during-reading activity above or you can select words for these activities. Possible words include *recipe, ingredients, formula, mayonnaise, speck, vinegar, juice, stir, amount, average,* and *mix*. Provide recipe cards on which students can copy the final drafts of their recipes and underline the vocabulary words.

New Word Swap
vocabulary reproducible for
Freckle Juice

Name_____ Date_____

Fill in just the first two columns below as you read the book. Then, exchange papers with a friend and fill in the third column.

New/confusing words	Sentence containing the word	Another word that would make sense in place of that word

Fluency Activities
for *Freckle Juice*

Pre-reading Activity: Tell students that in the book, Andrew buys a recipe for freckles. Ask students what a recipe is. Have students find recipes in magazines or cookbooks. Discuss how a recipe is written differently than a story or article. For example, point out that the ingredients are written in a list format rather than in sentences or paragraphs, the language is simple and to the point, etc. Tell students that a recipe is read very differently than a story, but it still must be read fluently. Demonstrate how a fluent reader would sound reading a recipe. Point out how you paused after each ingredient, even though there is no punctuation; you did not need to be overly expressive, because there is no emotion to express, but still did not read in a monotone voice; etc. Have each student select one recipe and practice reading it aloud in a fluent manner. Students may work in pairs or small groups.

During-reading Activity: The author, Judy Blume, often uses italics for emphasis. As you read the story, point out the italicized words. Have students notice how the words are "slanted" and tell them that type style is called *italics.* Explain that writers use italics so the reader knows which words to emphasize. Demonstrate this with the first sentence in which an italicized word is found: "What do you mean *how?* You get *born* with them. That's how!" (*Freckle Juice*, page 14). Have students reread the sentence, also stressing the italicized words. Use the next sentence on the same page with an italicized word ("Some help *he* was!") to demonstrate to students how different the sentence is when the word *he* is not emphasized. Explain that italicized words help a reader read fluently because they help him determine how dialogue should be said to show characters' emotions. Have students look for italicized words as they read the book, and practice reading these sentences fluently and with proper emphasis on the italicized words. Use the Emphasis Exercise reproducible (page 55) to practice reading italicized words. Students may work with partners by reading alternating sentences.

Post-reading Activity: Reread the first page of chapter 3 where Andrew says that he doesn't want to waste time getting home to read the recipe and that "he wasn't the world's fastest reader anyway, even though he'd gotten better since last fall" (*Freckle Juice*, page 26). Ask students if being the "world's fastest reader" would necessarily mean that a person is a good or fluent reader. Let students share their responses and reasoning. Then, tell students that you will read as fast as you can to see if Andrew is right—that being the "world's fastest reader" is a good thing. Read an excerpt from the book as fast as you possibly can. Ask students how that sounded. Was it easy to understand you? Did you sound natural? Was it interesting to listen to? Could you tell how the characters felt? Then, read the same excerpt at a normal pace. Ask students the same questions. Guide students toward concluding that being a fast reader is not necessarily the same as being a good reader. Students might enjoy repeating the same activity in pairs. Have them take turns reading the same excerpt as fast as possible and again at a normal, fluent pace.

Names _____ Date _____

Read the following sentences fluently. If you read with a partner, take turns reading every other sentence. Remember to stress or emphasize the words in italics. Notice how the italics help you read with expression.

"I wish *I* had freckles."

"*Freckles*? You mean you *want* freckles?"

"Of *course* I do! I mean, look at *you*. You've got them all *over*!"

"I know, and I *hate* them."

"You *what*? Why in the world would you hate your freckles? Freckles are the *coolest*!"

"*I* don't think so."

"Sure they are. I mean, they make you special and neat-looking. I have *nothing* that makes me look special."

"Yeah, *right*! You've got *curly hair*! I'd do *anything* to have curly hair."

"You *would*? Wow, I guess we all have *something* that makes us pretty special, huh?"

"Gee, I never thought of it *that* way. I guess you're right. My freckles *are* pretty cool."

Comprehension Activities
for *Freckle Juice*

Pre-reading Activity: Tell students that *Freckle Juice* is about a boy who wants to have freckles just like his classmate's. Ask each student to think of something he would like to change about himself, and write a journal entry describing what the trait is, why he would change it, and what he would be willing to do in order to change it. Ask volunteers to share their journal entries with partners or the class. To "break the ice" on this subject, you may want to write a journal entry of your own and share it with the class.

During-reading Activity: Tell students that good readers are always thinking as they read and that this is called *active reading*. Have students actively read the book by taking notes about the characters on copies of the Character Notes reproducible (page 57). Explain that many authors do not come right out and say what kind of person a character is because that would be boring. Instead, good authors "show, not tell" what a character is like with dialogue and actions. Tell students to watch for clues or proof that tells them what kind of people the main characters are and to list them on the chart under the corresponding character name. For example, students might notice and list that Sharon giggles when Andrew gets called to reading group, she makes up the recipe, and she makes frog faces. As the chart is completed, discuss with students what their notes say about the individual characters. Would they like to have these people in their class? Why or why not?

Post-reading Activity: Because this book is simple and relatively short, it lends itself well to this retelling activity. Bring in newspaper comic strips, and give students time to read them and notice their format. Have students retell the book in comic-strip format. Ask them to review the main events of the book and discuss which events are important enough to be included. Ask students to note the difference between main events and details. Have students work in pairs or independently to retell the book by writing and illustrating comic strips. Consider limiting the number of boxes used in the comic in order to ensure that students only include the most important events. Display on a bulletin board titled "Freckle Juice Funnies."

Character Notes
comprehension reproducible for
Freckle Juice

Names _____   Date _____

In each column, list details from the book that show what kind of characters Sharon, Miss Kelly, and Andrew are.

Sharon	Miss Kelly	Andrew

James and the Giant Peach
by Roald Dahl

(Alfred A. Knopf, 1961)

James Henry Trotter had a happy life until he was sent to live with his cruel aunts. But, when he dropped magic crystals by the peach tree, he found himself traveling inside a giant peach with some peculiar new friends. The story's plot, heavy dialogue, and short chapters help readers understand the challenging language.

Related books: *Alice's Adventures in Wonderland* by Lewis Carroll (Signet, 2000); *Charlie and the Chocolate Factory* by Roald Dahl (Puffin, 2002); *The Wonderful Wizard of Oz* by L. Frank Baum (HarperTrophy, 2001)

Phonemic Awareness Activities
for *James and the Giant Peach*

Pre-reading Activity: Ask what sound the letter s usually makes (/s/) and what sound it makes in James (/z/). The letter s usually makes the /s/ sound at the beginnings of words (exceptions: *sure, sugar*). At the end of a word, it can make the /s/ sound (like in *books*) or the /z/ sound (like in *hills*). If the consonant before the s is voiced, the s makes the /z/ sound. If the consonant is unvoiced, s makes the /s/ sound. A voiced consonant makes the vocal chords vibrate. An unvoiced consonant does not. The phoneme before the letter s in *James* is /m/. /M/ is voiced, so the s makes the /z/ sound. Have students place their hands on their throats and pronounce the phoneme /b/ and notice the vibration (/b/ is voiced). Then, have them pronounce the phoneme /p/ and notice there is no vibration (/p/ is voiceless). Have each student fold a piece of paper in half vertically, labeling one column *Voiced Consonants* and the other *Unvoiced Consonants*. Then, have them go through the alphabet, writing the phonemes for the graphemes. Have students write the phonemes under the appropriate columns. Demonstrate how to represent the sound of a letter with slashes: /b/. Use these lists to have students identify which sound the letter s makes in different words.

During-reading Activity: While reading the aunts' dueling poems on page 6, have students substitute other rhyming words and phrases leading up to them. For example, "I look and smell," Aunt Sponge declared, "as lovely as a rose! Just feast your eyes upon my face, observe my [wiggly toes]!" Do this activity orally, but consider recording some class responses and then rereading the poem in its entirety with the new rhymes.

Post-reading Activity: Play "Phoneme Bingo" using the Bingo Card reproducible (page 59). Have students randomly fill in the boxes on blank bingo cards with words from the story. Use torn paper for markers. Before playing, make a list of phonemic concepts relevant to students' abilities and needs. To play, call out a phonemic rule and have students mark words that fit that rule. For example, if you say "long /a/," students can mark *James*. If you say "consonant digraph," students can mark *earthworm* (th), *shark* (sh), and *peach* (ch). You can also use the phrasing, "Mark a word with the same initial phoneme as *giraffe*" (*James, giant*).

Bingo Card

phonemic awareness reproducible for
James and the Giant Peach

Name_____ Date_____

In any order, write the following words in the bingo spaces: *James, Henry, Trotter, giant, peach, tree, bag, magic, insects, aunt, Sponge, Spiker, rhinoceros, peculiar, crystals, grasshopper, ladybug, centipede, earthworm, spider, glowworm, sea, shark, silkworm,* and *cloud.*

Phoneme Bingo

Phonics Activities
for *James and the Giant Peach*

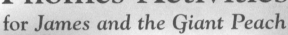re-reading Activity: Read the title to students. Ask what consonant phonemes they hear more than once (/j/). Then, ask students what letters represent this phoneme (J in *James*, G in *Giant*). Review that the phoneme /j/ can be made with the letter j or often with the letter g. When the letter g represents the /j/ sound, it is called soft g. Review with students what phonetic rule determines the sound the g makes. (If it is followed by e, i, or y, it is usually a soft g; otherwise it is usually a hard g.) Then, have students work in groups to brainstorm and list words containing the letters j and g. Have them sort words according to the sounds that the letter g makes.

uring-reading Activity: This activity provides a review of word families (onsets and rimes) and also helps students practice spelling rules. While reading, pause after the Centipede's first poem in chapter 14. Have students write new rhyming words for the poem. Point out to students that the words they write do not have to "go" in the poem, they simply have to rhyme with the original words. The catch is that they must be spelled correctly—many students at this level will spell every word using the same pattern. (For example, they will spell *beds* b-e-a-d-s for a list beginning with *heads* and *dreads*.) So, allow dictionary usage to check spelling. Also, allow students to rhyme words with either *dilemma* or *tremor*, since these two words are not exact rhymes. Have students use the Games and the Giant Beach reproducible (page 61) on the following page to build and list new words that go with each of the rhyming words in the poem. Give each student one point for each correctly spelled word, and no points for misspelled words. Challenge students to list the greatest number of real words for each rime. Consider doing this in teams and awarding teams points for each original correctly spelled word, then reward the teams with one minute of extra free time per point.

ost-reading Activity: Roald Dahl uses many poems throughout the book to express the characters' feelings and thoughts. The aunts use poetry to have a "duel" about who is more beautiful. The Centipede uses rhyming songs at various times throughout the book, and James uses a poem to introduce his friends to the city of New York. Have students reread these poems to "get the feel" of them. Then, have students write rhyming poems about the book *James and the Giant Peach*. The poems can be similar to the one James recites in that they can describe all of the characters, they can be summaries of the story itself, or they can describe scenes from the book. Consider pairing students to complete the activity so that they can brainstorm rhyming words together. When the first drafts are complete, have students review them and look for any misspellings or rhyming errors. After students have corrected their papers, have them rewrite and illustrate the poems. Bind the pages together into a class book called *Peachy Poetry*. Place the book in a center and let students take turns looking for the rhyming words.

Games and the Giant Beach

phonics reproducible for
James and the Giant Peach

Name_____ Date_____

How many words can you think of that rhyme with the Centipede's rhymes in his poem in chapter 14 (*James and the Giant Peach,* pages 40-41)? The words do not have to make sense in the poem; they just have to rhyme. Only correctly spelled words will receive points! Use the back of your paper for more space.

heads dreads	snow blow	scrunch lunch	bite night	knows toes	there hair	hen then

bred head	see knee	gnat hat	frost tossed	tremor dilemma	hill until	plunge sponge

Vocabulary Activities
for *James and the Giant Peach*

Pre-reading Activity: Teach the concept of *fantasy*. Have a volunteer look up the word in a dictionary and read the definition to the class. List some of the characteristics that make a book a fantasy. Have students give examples of fantasy elements and list these on a chart. Show the cover of the book to students and ask them what elements can be added to the chart (giant peach, giant bugs wearing clothing and talking, etc.). Tell students that as they read the book, they will add to the "fantasy chart" by listing elements they find in the reading that make this book a fantasy.

During-reading Activity: Students will encounter many new and interesting words while reading the book. Tell students that pausing to look up each one during the reading would interrupt the reading flow too much. Discuss what else can be done and suggest using context clues for some words. Then, put students in charge of teaching each other some of the vocabulary words encountered in the book. Give each student a few sticky notes and direct them to select one word per chapter (or few chapters) he would like to learn and teach to the rest of the class. When a student encounters a new, interesting word, instruct him to mark the page with a sticky note. (Each student may initially mark more than one word, but for practicality, he should choose only one word for the group work.) Assign students to groups. After the day's reading, instruct each group to share the words chosen during independent reading and vote on one to present to the class. Have each group look up the word in a dictionary, decide on its meaning as it is used in the story, and write a new sentence using the word. After all of the groups have completed the assignment, ask groups to present their vocabulary words, definitions, and new sentences to the class. As each new word is presented, let each student copy every new word, definition, and sentence on a set of index cards. At the end of reading *James and the Giant Peach*, the class will have student-created vocabulary word cards to be used for other activities or tests.

Post-reading Activity: Have students turn to the scene in chapter 23 when the shipmen have seen James and the peach: ". . . a giant ladybug . . . a colossal green grasshopper . . . a mammoth spider . . . an enormous centipede." (*James and the Giant Peach*, pages 74-75). Have students notice how many different words the sailor used to describe the bugs: *giant, colossal, mammoth, enormous*. Ask students what those words mean (*big*). Remind students that these are synonyms. Explain that they will be using interesting synonyms to describe the characters in the book, much in the way the shipmen did. Give each student a copy of the James and the Giant, Colossal, Mammoth, Enormous Peach reproducible (page 63). Instruct each student to begin by drawing each character and writing one word to describe that character. Challenge students to use different adjectives for each character. Then, have students list synonyms for each of the adjectives. For example, a student might list *James: smart, intelligent, bright, sharp, clever, gifted, advanced, brilliant*. Provide a thesaurus for every three or four students, if possible. Encourage students to refer back to the book for ideas. (The poem James uses to introduce his friends to New York might be particularly helpful.) Display the student work on a bulletin board titled "Characters from James and the Giant, Colossal, Mammoth, Enormous Peach."

James and the Giant, Colossal, Mammoth, Enormous Peach
vocabulary reproducible for
James and the Giant Peach

Name_____ Date_____

In each column, list one adjective that describes the character. Then, list synonyms for the adjectives in the columns.

James	Aunt Spiker	Aunt Sponge	Grasshopper	Spider

Earthworm	Centipede	Silkworm	Glowworm	Ladybug

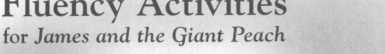

Fluency Activities
for *James and the Giant Peach*

Pre-reading Activity: Use the blurb on the back cover of *James and the Giant Peach* to practice fluency and preview the book. Have students listen as you read the blurb aloud. Next, have students write predictions based on the blurb. Encourage students to answer specific questions such as "What kind of adventure will James have? What are some of the things that might happen? Where does the peach go?" Then, have students read their predictions aloud to partners. Remind students to speak clearly and at "normal" speed. Their words should flow smoothly and fluently, the way they would if students were talking.

During-reading Activity: The poems in this book are excellent tools for fluency practice. Each time you encounter a poem in the reading, read it twice more aloud. Tell students to follow along and notice your voice intonations, expressions, etc. The second time, have students echo read and mimic the fluent reading. The third time, have students read it chorally without you. Usually, it is at this point when students will slow down and become very "robotic" and "chant-y." This is an automatic reaction in an attempt to keep up with everyone. When this occurs, pause and point this out. Remind students that they should sound natural and fluent—not "sing-songy," so that the emphasis is on the meaning in the poem as well as its rhythm. Last, have students read the poems aloud to each other and to small groups. Consider having volunteers read aloud to the class after a few days of at-home practice. Encourage students to add "dramatic flair."

Post-reading Activity: It is important for students to learn that readers become more fluent with practice, and that the more familiar they are with material, the more fluently they will read it. In order to demonstrate this, have each student select a scene to read aloud to a partner. Instruct students to only read their scenes aloud one time to their partners and not practice or review them. After the first student has finished reading her selection aloud, ask the second student to rate the reader's fluency using the Rate My Reading reproducible (page 65). Next, the second student should read a different scene and have the first student rate his fluency using the Rate My Reading reproducible (page 65). Then, have partners split up and quietly reread their selections aloud repeatedly, each time attempting to improve fluency. After several minutes of practice, have the partners reconvene and repeat the original process. Regroup as a class and discuss observations and assessment sheets. Show how different the assessments are the second time around, after each partner has had an opportunity to practice.

Rate My Reading

fluency reproducible for
James and the Giant Peach

Listen to your partner read a scene from *James and the Giant Peach*. Circle the responses below that best describe how fluently your partner reads.

My name: _____ My partner's name: _____ Pages read:___

First Read-Aloud Assessment

My partner's voice was loud and clear.   yes   no   somewhat

My partner knew almost every single word.   yes   no

My partner sounded very natural, just   yes   no   somewhat
as if he or she were talking normally.

My partner was very expressive.   yes   no   somewhat

My partner paused at punctuation.   yes   no   somewhat

My partner did not repeat anything.   yes   no

Second Read-Aloud Assessment

My partner's voice was loud and clear.   yes   no   somewhat

My partner knew almost every single word.   yes   no

My partner sounded very natural, just   yes   no   somewhat
as if he or she were talking normally.

My partner was very expressive.   yes   no   somewhat

My partner paused at punctuation.   yes   no   somewhat

My partner did not repeat anything.   yes   no

Here is what I noticed about my partner's reading after he or she practiced: _____

_____

_____

_____

Comprehension Activities
for *James and the Giant Peach*

Pre-reading Activity: Read only the first page to students (which introduces James and explains how his parents were eaten by an angry rhinoceros). Have students respond to the page in writing by making predictions and answering some of the following questions: "What do you think about the first scene? Why did the author make their accident so unusual? What do you think will happen to James now? How do you feel for James? Where do you think James will go?" If some students have read the book before, assign them the task of reading the predictions and drawing smiley faces next to correct guesses. Return papers to students after you finish reading the book as a class.

During-reading Activity: Point out to students that even though the characters are animals, Roald Dahl has given them human-like characteristics and distinct personalities. For example, in chapter 13 (*James and the Giant Peach*, page 34) when the Centipede says "For goodness' sake, stop staring round the room and get on with my boots! And kindly line them up neatly in pairs as you take them off. Don't just throw them over your shoulder" as James frantically tries to take off the many boots, the author shows that the Centipede can be rude and selfish. Explain that giving animals human traits is called *anthropomorphism*. Have students monitor their comprehension and the development of characters with copies of the Character-Istics reproducible (page 67). As students proceed through the book and learn more about the animals, have students add to the reproducibles. Discuss how certain behaviors and statements help the reader get to know each animal's personality. Note that, like the illustrations on the worksheet, the animals would be just plain animals without the author to give them personalities.

Post-reading Activity: Have students review the sequence of events in the book by creating a mural time line depicting the peach's travels. Begin by reviewing and listing all of the places the peach went, starting with the peach tree in the aunts' yard. Have students take notes about what happened at each location. Then, have students create a time line on a large sheet of bulletin board paper by drawing the peach in its locations, along with details such as the characters involved and what happened. Provide paint, glitter, and other supplies to make the mural particularly detailed. For example, consider using orange felt to depict the peach, chenille craft sticks for the insects' antennae, blue cellophane for the sea, etc. Tell students that once the mural is complete, someone who has never read the book should be able to see a summary of it by looking at the mural. Display the mural on a wall in the classroom or in a hallway.

Character-Istics

comprehension reproducible for

James and the Giant Peach

Name_____ Date_____

As you read the book, monitor the characters' development by recording information you learn about the insects. Think about how their actions tell what their personalities are like. Write what you learn about each character's personality on this sheet.

Silkworm personality traits

Ladybug personality traits

Spider personality traits

Earthworm personality traits

Grasshopper personality traits

Glowworm personality traits

Centipede personality traits

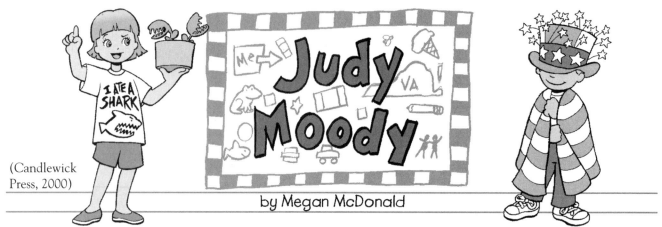

(Candlewick Press, 2000)

by Megan McDonald

Judy Moody is always in a mood—sometimes good, but often bad! The story starts with Judy waking up for the first day of third grade which, despite her fears, might not be so bad after all. The dialogue is funny, clever, and realistic. The book lends itself to character analysis, authentic fluency practice, and natural phonics activities.

Related books: *Horrible Harry Moves Up to Third Grade* by Suzy Kline (Puffin, July 2000); *Judy Moody Gets Famous!* by Megan McDonald (Candlewick Press, 2003); *Judy Moody Saves the World* by Megan McDonald (Candlewick Press, 2002)

Phonemic Awareness Activities
for *Judy Moody*

Pre-reading Activity: Read the back cover aloud. On the board, write "Judy Moody was in a mood. Not a good mood. A bad mood."
Ask students to repeat the sentences, and ask where they hear the /oo/ sound (*Judy, Moody, mood*). (Some phonics programs consider this the long /u/ sound.) Have them identify which graphemes represent the /oo/ sound in each word (u and oo). Ask, "Do the letters oo in *good* also make the same /oo/ sound as in *Judy, Moody,* and *mood*? To practice listening for the /oo/ sounds, have each student write *Judy Moody* on one index card and *good* on another. Say an /oo/ word. Each student should hold up a Judy Moody card or a good card, depending on which sound she hears. Possible words to use for Judy Moody are *flew, moon, rude, blue, true, news, bloom, juice, glue, threw, fruit, cruise,* and *moo*. Possible words to use for good are *book, look, took, brook, hook, hoof, wood, push,* and *stood*.

During-reading Activity: Judy Moody says the word *roar* to express displeasure and *rare* to express delight. When you encounter *roar* in chapter 1, ask students to "roar," then divide the word into phonemes (/r/ and /or/). The final phoneme (represented by the letters oar), is an r-controlled or murmur diphthong (a vowel followed by an r); the letter r "controls" the vowel sound. This is also called "bossy r" because the r "tells" the vowel what sound to make. Give other examples of words containing the bossy /r/ sound, and have students identify and repeat them. Then, have students look for other r-controlled/bossy /r/ sounds as they continue reading. Whenever students hear a bossy-r word, let them "roar."

Post-reading Activity: Review chapter 4. Discuss why Judy's dad agreed so readily to go to the pet store. (He needed a five-letter word for fish that started with the letter m to complete his crossword puzzle.) Give each student a copy of the Judy Moody Crossword reproducible (page 69). Have students complete the crossword puzzles just like Judy's dad, using the phonemic clues given.

Judy Moody Crossword

phonemic awareness reproducible for
Judy Moody

Name_____ Date_____

Read the crossword puzzle clues and fill in the crossword puzzle.

DOWN
1. One of Judy's favorite words. It means things are great and contains a "bossy r."
3. Judy's teacher's name; it rhymes with the first syllable in the word *body.*
5. Judy's little brother whose name starts with the /st/ blend.
7. Judy's brother dressed up as this, and it starts with the /fl/ blend.
9. Two letters that stand for the name of the club to which Judy and her friends belong. These letters make the beginning and ending sounds in the word "top."

ACROSS
2. Judy's favorite pet. Its name rhymes with *pause.*
4. Judy's other pet. Her name ends with a silent e.
6. Judy's often in this mood; it rhymes with *glad.*
7. One of Judy's two friends from her class. This friend has only one syllable and two blends in his name.
8. Judy thought of this word for the spelling activity in chapter 2. It contains a g that makes no sound (is silent).

Phonics Activities
for *Judy Moody*

Pre-reading Activity: Show the title to students and ask them if the letter y is used as a consonant or a vowel in the words *Judy Moody* (vowel). Tell students that they will discover the phonetic rule for when the letter y is a consonant (/y/ sound) and for when it is used as a vowel. (It makes the long /e/ sound or the long /i/ sound, and occasionally the short /i/ sound, as in *gypsy* and *myth*.) Have students brainstorm words containing the letter y. Students can brainstorm in small groups, or they can use text from the book, newspapers, magazines, etc., to find words. Have each student list words in three columns with the headings *y as a consonant*, *y as the long /e/ sound*, and *y as the long /i/ sound*. As students' lists grow, have them look for phonetic patterns to discover and name the phonetic y rule. (When the letter y begins a word or syllable, it usually makes its consonant /y/ sound; otherwise, the letter y makes a vowel sound.) After students have discovered this rule, challenge them to figure out the pattern for the long /e/ and long /i/ sounds; usually a final y on a word with two or more syllables will make the long /e/ sound (*party, happy, nursery*) while a final y in a one-syllable word will usually make the long /i/ sound (*cry, by, try*).

During-reading Activity: Pause after reading chapter 2 and review how Judy changed Mr. Todd's name on the first day of school. (She called him Mr. Toad.) Write the two words on the board and ask students to identify what letters are changed and how the change affects the word. (The first d was changed to the letter a which turned the short /o/ sound to a long /o/ sound.) Tell students that this is a good example of how important spelling is; one simple letter can completely change a word's pronunciation and its meaning. Explain that the reason the word changed into a long vowel sound is because the word *toad* has a vowel team. Tell students that when two vowels are together, usually the "first one does the talking while the second one keeps walking." Have students cut out the letters on copies of the We Are a Team! reproducible (page 71) to form words. Then, direct each student to change or add a letter in a word to see how it changes. For example, say, "What do you spell when you put together the g, o, and t letter cards? Right, got. What sounds do you hear in this word? Right, /g/, /o/, /t/. Now, slip the a letter card between the o and the t. How does the word change? Yes, now you have *goat*. The vowel sound has changed to a long /o/. Why?" Other possible word combinations could be *gal/goal, bat/bait, bat/boat, bed/bead, bet/beat, bat/beat, led/lead, lid/lied, rod/road, red/read, hat/heat, her/hear, met or mat/meat, mat/moat,* and *cat/coat*. Note that *lead* and *read* can maintain their original pronunciations as well.

Post-reading Activity: Have students look through the book to find reasons why Judy ended up liking Mr. Todd. (He ordered pizza on the first day, let her have the "pizza table," had an interesting spelling activity, etc.). Ask students to find the part in chapter 2 when the class does the spelling activity with the words *Gino's Extra-Cheese Pizza*. Remind students that Mr. Todd asked his class to come up with five words. Challenge your students to come up with as many words as they can from these letters in an allotted time. Then, award the student who comes up with the most correctly spelled words and the one who comes up with the longest word.

We Are a Team!

phonics reproducible for
Judy Moody

Name_____ Date _____

Cut out the letter cards. Make as many three letter words as you can think of. Each time you make a word, add a vowel to act as a team with the vowel that is already in the word to create a new word. Common vowel teams are oa, ea, and ai. Notice how adding, changing, or taking away one letter can completely change a word.

g	o	t	a	l	b	i

e	r	d	f	m	h	c

Vocabulary Activities
for *Judy Moody*

Pre-reading Activity: Read the blurb on the back cover of *Judy Moody* and discuss what *moods* are. Tell students that Judy Moody often behaves as if she is in a bad mood, even when she is secretly in a good mood. For example, when she goes to school on the first day, she is in a bad mood, but then her teacher assigns some fun activities, and she starts to get excited. Instead of showing her excitement, however, Judy continues to behave as if she is in a bad mood! Tell students to watch for "opposite behaviors" when they start reading the book. Ask students what it might mean to be in a "good" mood. Then, ask students what it might mean to be in the opposite mood. Tell students that another word for opposites is *antonyms*. Tell students that you will give an example of a "good mood behavior," and they will say what the opposite is. For example, Judy smiles/frowns; Judy is happy/sad; etc. After a few responses, have each student complete the Good and Bad Moods reproducible (page 73) by filling in the antonym for each listed word. Then, have students add illustrations for each pair.

During-reading Activity: Tell students that Megan McDonald uses *similes* in her writing. Explain that similes use the words *as* or *like* to compare two nouns in a sentence. Give an example from the book such as "Judy rolled her tongue like a hot dog" (*Judy Moody*, page 22). As you read the book, have students keep lists of similes they encounter. At the end of each chapter, have students share any similes they found. After completing the book, have each student select her favorite simile from the book, write it on a sheet of white construction paper, and illustrate it. Underneath the similes, have students write *by Megan McDonald*. Then, have each student write her own simile on the back of the paper, and sign her name. Have students illustrate their similes as well. Then, collect all of the individual pages and bind them into a class book titled *Similes by Megan McDonald and Us!*

Post-reading Activity: Refer to chapter 2, when Judy uses four spelling words in one sentence; "The tiger spit on the rat and the gnat." (*Judy Moody*, page 28). Challenge students to write sentences using as many vocabulary words as possible. Tell students that although the sentences can be silly, like Judy's, they must make sense. Be sure students know the meanings of the words prior to allowing them to work independently. Note that some words, such as *rare, roar,* and *cracked,* are used as idioms. Possible vocabulary words to use from the book are *mood, grouchy, rare, roar, glared, cracked, secretly, surveyed, collage, dangled, sparkle, favorite, worst, collapsing, lodged, twisted, hobbies, collecting, dare,* and *wrecked*.

Good and Bad Moods
vocabulary reproducible for
Judy Moody

Name_____ Date_____

Sometimes Judy Moody behaves in the opposite way of how she feels. If she is secretly in a happy mood about something, she will often behave like she is in a bad mood! Fill in the blanks below with words that mean the opposite of the words listed. Then, illustrate the antonym pairs.

open _____   laughing _____

huge _____   smooth _____

under _____   dark _____

Fluency Activities
for *Judy Moody*

Pre-reading Activity: Tell students that the main character in the book, Judy Moody, is a feisty girl with a bit of an "attitude." Although she is never really rude to anyone, she is not afraid to show her bad moods—especially with her little brother, Stink. Ask students how they think a reader should sound when reading aloud dialogue from a character like Judy. Would the reader's voice be soft, slow, and shy? Would the reader's voice be strong and sometimes grouchy? Ask students to role-play what an older, moody sister might sound like when talking to a little brother who broke her new toy. Remind students that part of being a fluent reader is to be "true" to the character's voice and personality. Tell students to keep this in mind as they read or hear the book.

During-reading Activity: While reading chapter 5, pause at "'Here you go,' she said in her best squeaky baby voice. 'You like ants, don't you?'" (*Judy Moody*, page 61). Reread that sentence and ask students to try reading Judy's dialogue in a squeaky, baby voice. Discuss why they think the author chose to add this to the writing. Point out to students that by stating what kind of voice Judy used when speaking to the plant, the reader is better able to tell what Judy is thinking and feeling. Throughout the reading, pause in similar situations such as when Judy is in a bad mood, is hanging up the phone with Frank Pearl, or when she is angry with Stink. Take time out from the reading to focus on how the character's dialogue should be read in a fluent and realistic manner that would be appropriate for the scene.

Post-reading Activity: Reread the part in the book when Judy presents her collage to the class. Ask students if they think Judy spoke in a dull, shy, monotone voice, or in a proud, self-confident, excited voice. Ask students which "voice" would be more interesting to listen to. Tell students that they will have an opportunity to present Me Collages—just like Judy's—to the class and at the same time, they will get to practice their fluency. Assign a Me Collage like the one Mr. Todd had his class do in the book. Tell students that on the project's due date they will have to present their collages to the class as well, but will be allowed to read from notes. Stress to students that they will be assessed not only on their projects, but on their presentations—how well they speak to the class. Will they be clear and easily understood? Will they read their notes in a fluent manner that shows they rehearsed? Will they be expressive and exciting to listen to? Use the Me Collage reproducible (page 75) as a guide for students' presentations.

Me Collage

fluency reproducible for
Judy Moody

Name _____ Date _____

You will be doing a Me Collage, just like Judy. Your collage will have the same categories that Judy's did:
* Who I am
* Where I live
* My friends
* My best friend
* My favorite pet
* When I grow up
* Hobbies
* The worst thing that ever happened to me
* The funniest thing that ever happened to me
* Clubs

After completing your collage, prepare a short speech for your presentation to the class. Practice reading your speech aloud several times so that you are prepared. We want to hear fluent readers!

Your speech will be evaluated on the following:
* Are you reading in a loud, clear voice?
* Do you sound excited, confident, and prepared?
* Can we tell you rehearsed?
* Are you reading the words smoothly, without stumbling or getting stuck?
* Are you reading at a comfortable speed?
* Are you pausing where commas and periods should be?
* Do you sound expressive—not like a robot?
* Are you chunking words together appropriately, or do you sound choppy?
* Do you sound natural, the way you do when you talk?

Comprehension Activities
for *Judy Moody*

Pre-reading Activity: Tell students that this book has some peculiar chapter titles. Have students read the table of contents and make predictions for each chapter. Point out to students how some of the chapter names "build" on each other such as "My Favorite Pet" and then "My Smelly Pet." Tell students that it is very helpful to use all available information prior to reading a book for predictions because predictions set a purpose for reading. Explain that setting a purpose is like "getting your brain ready"—like a warm-up. Tell students that if their brains know a little bit about what to expect, it will help them understand the book better. Encourage students to add or change their predictions prior to each new chapter.

During-reading Activity: This graphic organizer activity helps students monitor their comprehension as they proceed through the reading, and also lets them interact with and relate to the literature, use compare-and-contrast strategies, and get to know the main character better. Have students compare themselves to Judy Moody as they learn about her. Give each student a copy of the Judy and Me reproducible (page 77) to record information she learns about Judy and compare it to things she knows about herself. Encourage students to include information such as grade level, family life, pets, what they want to be when they grow up, hobbies, collections, etc. Instruct each student to list Judy's differences in the circle next to the box that is labeled *Judy Moody*, and her own differences in the circle next to the box labeled *You*. Each student should list similarities in the overlapping section of the two circles.

Post-reading Activity: Review chapter 10, when Judy has a terrible day in school; "In Spelling, Judy wrote WEASELS when Mr. Todd had really said MEASLES. In Science, when Jessica Finch threw Judy the ball of yarn for their giant spiderweb, she dropped it. It rolled out the door just when Ms. Tuxedo, the principal, walked past in high heels" (*Judy Moody*, page 120). Tell students that they will have an opportunity to make a giant spiderweb, like Judy's class. The two differences will be that it won't be for a science lesson, and hopefully, no one will drop the yarn and have it roll out for the principal to trip on! Instead, students will use the web to take turns reviewing the main events in the book. Give students a few minutes to skim the book and review the most important events. List the chapter titles on the board as a reference. Have students stand in a circle in the middle of the classroom. Join them in the circle with a ball of yarn. Begin the web by naming the first main event that happens in the book. (Judy wakes up in a bad mood on the first day of third grade.) Then, hold onto the strand of yarn and toss the yarn ball to another student in the circle. Have that student name the next major event that occurred, hold onto the strand of yarn, and then toss the ball of yarn to someone else. Ask the next person to name the next major event, hold onto the yarn, and toss the ball to the next person. Continue until all of the main events have been named in order to create a "spiderweb." Discuss how, although the web might look confusing, it can be traced from beginning to end, or vice versa, because all of the events connect to each other in a sequence.

Judy and Me
comprehension reproducible for
Judy Moody

Name _____ Date _____

Compare yourself to Judy Moody. How are you alike? How are you different? Write characteristics that only you have in the top section of the top circle. Write characteristics that only Judy has in the bottom section of the bottom circle. In the section where the two circles overlap, write things you have in common with Judy. Draw a self-portrait in the box labeled *You*.

You

Judy Moody

The Legend of the Indian Paintbrush

by Tomie dePaola

(G. P. Putnam's Sons, 1988)

This book retells the Texas legend of the Indian paintbrush flower's origin. Little Gopher, a Native American boy, tenaciously follows his Dream-Vision and fulfills his destiny: to paint his people's deeds and the colors of the sunset.

Related books: *The Girl Who Loved Wild Horses* by Paul Goble (Scott Foresman, 1993); *The Legend of the Bluebonnet* by Tomie dePaola (Paper Star, 1996); *The Legend of the Poinsettia* by Tomie dePaola (Paper Star, 1997); *Rainbow Crow: A Lenape Tale* by Nancy Van Laan (Knopf, 1991)

Phonemic Awareness Activities
for *The Legend of the Indian Paintbrush*

Pre-reading Activity: Write the story words from the Answer Key (page 158) on index cards. Tell students that the main character is a painter. Ask what phoneme the letters ai make in the word *paint* (long /a/). Explain that other graphemes can make the long /a/ sound. Have students sit in a circle. Spread the cards faceup in the center. Give one student a paintbrush. Then, have him choose a card, read the word, and identify the letters making the long /a/ sound. (Not all words will have the long /a/ sound.) If the student answers correctly, let him keep the card, and pass the paintbrush to another student. If he chooses incorrectly, have him give the paintbrush to you. Then, select the next player. At the end of the game, have students read their cards aloud for review.

During-reading Activity: This is an excellent book to teach or reinforce hard and soft g. Ask, "What is the middle consonant sound in the word *legend* (/j/)?" Repeat with the character's name, *Gopher*. Tell students that the /j/ sound in *legend* is the soft g sound, while the /g/ sound in *Gopher* is the hard /g/ sound. As you read the story, have students identify any hard and soft g sounds they hear by calling out the corresponding sound. Then, have pairs identify the hard and soft g sounds in the word list on the Hard and Soft G Sounds reproducible (page 79).

Post-reading Activity: Use *The Legend of the Indian Paintbrush* to teach the consonant digraph /ng/ with focus on the inflectional ending of word variants. Reread lines 6-9 of page 1. Ask what sounds students hear at the end of the words *riding, running, shooting,* and *wrestling.* Say the phoneme /ng/. Have students repeat. Reread lines 6-9 and ask them to listen for the /ng/ phoneme in a different word (*strength*). Explain that although the phoneme is the same in all five words, the /ng/ is heard in the first four due to the inflectional ending (adding ing to the root words). Brainstorm other words that contain the /ng/ phoneme. List responses on a two-column chart labeled *Words ending in /ng/* and *Words containing /ng/.*

Hard and Soft G Sounds

phonemic awareness reproducible for
The Legend of the Indian Paintbrush

Name_____ Date_____

Fold your paper in half. Call out the words on one side of the page to a partner. Have your partner tell you whether the letter g in each word makes a hard or soft sound. Circle hard or soft next to each word, then review the answers. The correct answer is next to each word, but do not share the answers until your partner has finished. Then, let your partner call out the words on the other side of the page to you.

ago /g/	hard soft	grandfather /g/ hard soft
legend /j/	hard soft	great /g/ hard soft
growth /g/	hard soft	page /j/ hard soft
agent /j/	hard soft	gathered /g/ hard soft
gymnasium /j/	hard soft	go /g/ hard soft
gelatin /j/	hard soft	package /j/ hard soft
angel /j/	hard soft	general /j/ hard soft
alligator /g/	hard soft	dragon /g/ hard soft
forget /g/	hard soft	gypsy /j/ hard soft
flag /g/	hard soft	gave /g/ hard soft
cage /j/	hard soft	ground /g/ hard soft
manager /j/	hard soft	gaze /g/ hard soft
brag /g/	hard soft	gem /j/ hard soft
game /g/	hard soft	engine /j/ hard soft
age /j/	hard soft	genuine /j/ hard soft
giraffe /j/	hard soft	ghost /g/ hard soft
garden /g/	hard soft	gorilla /g/ hard soft
magazine /g/	hard soft	imagination /j/ hard soft
ranger /j/	hard soft	haggle /g/ hard soft
beg /g/	hard soft	strange /j/ hard soft
gopher /g/	hard soft	gain /g/ hard soft
gift /g/	hard soft	gasoline /g/ hard soft
image /j/	hard soft	genetic /j/ hard soft
giggle /g/	hard soft	gentle /j/ hard soft
cabbage /j/	hard soft	pigeon /j/ hard soft
geology /j/	hard soft	wagon /g/ hard soft
twig /g/	hard soft	boggle /g/ hard soft
danger /j/	hard soft	stage /j/ hard soft

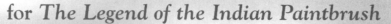

Phonics Activities
for *The Legend of the Indian Paintbrush*

re-reading Activity: Read the title aloud to students, then write the word *paintbrush* on the board. Ask, "What is the first vowel sound in the word *paintbrush?*" Students will answer that it is a long /a/ sound. Then, ask what other letters can make the long /a/ sound (ea, a_e, ay, etc.). Tell students to watch for other long /a/ words as they read the story or listen for them as you read it aloud. Consider putting the long /a/ words from the book on a word wall or on a spelling list, so that students can compare the various ways to make the long /a/ sound.

uring-reading Activity: This activity correlates to the phonemic awareness during-reading activity (page 78). As students read *The Legend of the Indian Paintbrush*, have them look for and list all of the words containing the letter g and sort them into hard and soft g sounds. (Note that students may list words containing the ng consonant digraph pattern. When this occurs, teach or review that the letters n and g represent one grapheme and consequently one sound—thus, these words do not fall under hard or soft g. Or, you can let students sort the ng words where they think they belong, and lead them to discover the differences between hard and soft g and ng digraph later in the lesson. Make similar adjustments if students notice any silent g's.) Tell students that their challenge is to discover the phonetic rule that applies to hard and soft g by using their sorted word lists. Have students list and sort other words containing the letter g. They can find these words in other books, magazines, newspapers, or the Hard and Soft G Sounds reproducible (page 79). As students' hard and soft g lists become longer, they should begin to see the pattern: g usually makes the hard /g/ sound when followed by any letter except e, i, or y; when the letter g is followed by e, i, or y, it is usually the /j/ sound. When a student thinks he has discovered the pattern that explains the hard and soft g rule, ask him to explain it. Discuss the student's rationale for the argument, possible exceptions, etc.

ost-reading Activity: Reread lines 6-9 of page 1 of the story and have students identify the ing verbs. List the words *riding, running,* and *wrestling* on the board and ask students to identify the base word for each. Then, ask students what they notice about the beginning sound for each of these words. (The /r/ sound is at the beginnings.) Next, ask what students notice about the beginning of the word *wrestling* when they compare it to *riding* and *running.* Explain that some words have a silent w in front of the r, but still make the /r/ sound. Brainstorm a list of silent w words on the board. Have students complete copies of the Silent W reproducible (page 81) for additional review.

Silent W

phonics reproducible for
The Legend of the Indian Paintbrush

Name_____ Date_____

Write a silent w word for each definition. Add wr to the words from the word bank, then write them in the correct blanks.

_____ a small, brown songbird

_____ the joint between the hand and arm

_____ to put words on paper

_____ incorrect

_____ a tool used to tighten or loosen bolts

_____ a paper cover around a book, or a plastic cover around candy

_____ to crash a car or to destroy something

_____ a circle of greenery often hung on doors or in windows

_____ a crease in skin, paper, or fabric

Word Bank

_ _ong   _ _eath   _ _apper   _ _inkle   _ _ite

_ _ench   _ _ist   _ _eck   _ _en

Vocabulary Activities
for *The Legend of the Indian Paintbrush*

Pre-reading Activity: Because the concept of a legend is critical to the understanding of this book, it is important to review this word. Prior to reading the book, have students begin KWL charts on legends, or start a class KWL chart on chart paper. Divide the paper into three columns. Label the first column *K—What I* Know *about Legends*. Label the second column *W—What I* Want *To Know about Legends*. Label the third column *L—What I* Learned *about Legends*. Have each student complete the first two columns of his chart, and then discuss students' prior knowledge about legends, and what they hope to learn from this book. As you read the story, have students keep the KWL charts in mind so that they can confirm or correct their existing knowledge on legends, as well as possibly answer questions from their W columns. After reading the book, discuss and let students add to the L columns of the charts. Have students research legends using dictionaries, the Internet, and other sources. Then, complete the chart. Compare and discuss how their understanding of the word *legend* has grown.

During-reading Activity: This activity teaches one of the story's vocabulary words (*shaman*), and also informs students of how to use context clues while reading. As you read the book, pause on the second page and think aloud, "*Shaman*. . . hmm, I have never heard that word before, and I'm not really sure what it means. What do you think we should do?" Discuss with the class what a reader can do when she discovers an unknown word. When the option "Look it up in a dictionary" is offered, ask students, "But, what can I do if the word is not in the dictionary? Or, if I don't have a dictionary nearby? Or, if I don't want to interrupt my reading experience to use a dictionary?" Guide students to find clues in the reading that will help them figure out the meaning of the word *shaman* (picture clues, text clues such as "wise shaman of the tribe" (*The Legend of the Indian Paintbrush*, page 3), prior knowledge about Native Americans, etc.). After agreeing on a satisfactory definition for the word *shaman*, tell students that what they just did is called using context clues and can be used at any time, with any word, and with any book.

Post-Reading Activity: Write the words *paintbrush* and *sunset* on the board and ask students what the words have in common. (They are compound words.) Review that a *compound word* is a word that is made when two words are put together to form a new word. Divide each word into its two smaller words. Have students reread the story to find and list all of the compound words. This can be done as a class as you read aloud or in groups with multiple copies of the book. Students can also find compound words in other books, newspapers, magazines, etc., and brainstorm new compound words. Play "Compound Competition." Call out a word such as *door*, and have students list as many compound words as they can think of that go with the word (*doorway, doorknob, doorstop*, etc.). Then, let students use the Compound Memory reproducible (page 83) to play another game.

First-Rate Reading™ Grade 3 • CD-0071 • © Carson-Dellosa

Compound Memory
vocabulary reproducible for
The Legend of the Indian Paintbrush

Name_____ Date_____

Cut out the word cards below. Shuffle cards and place them facedown on a flat surface. Flip over the cards to find the matches that make compound words. When you find a matching pair, keep it and take another turn. Some words have more than one match, so use the book to help you find the right words and end up with no extra cards. The player with the most pairs wins.

ground	sun	hill	down
home	play	good	room
side	under	paint	skin
work	under	set	stairs
brush	class	bye	buck

re-reading Activity: This book is an excellent tool for teaching "chunking" because the sentences are written in lines rather than paragraphs. Show students the text on some of the pages and ask, "How is this book written differently than other books you have read? What does the text look like?" Many students will say it looks like a poem. After students have identified that the text is written line by line instead of in paragraphs, ask them to list possible reasons why the author might have chosen to do this. Read the first page aloud and point out how the text structure dictates the pace of your reading. Tell students that dePaola's style helps the reader be more fluent because it shows which words should be chunked together. For example, say, "When you read the first line, 'Many years ago,' do you read those words together in a chunk, or group, and take a very short pause before continuing to the next line? Do you think Tomie dePaola wrote it this way on purpose to help us find the rhythm of his story?" Encourage students to listen for this rhythm when you read aloud. See the fluency post-reading activity for an extension of this activity.

uring-reading Activity: Because of its length, this activity works especially well with *The Legend of the Indian Paintbrush*. The book is short enough so that the activity is practical, but still has enough text to make it meaningful. (Students can practice fluency with the entire text.) Assign students to pairs or small groups, depending on how many copies of the book are available. Read each page aloud in a fluent, expressive voice. Then, have one student (the reader) in each pair or group repeat the page for the listener(s). Instruct the readers to try to "copy" the manner in which you read, and the listeners to provide feedback and praise. It may be helpful for students to role-play this type of reading prior to beginning the class activity. Continue reading each page aloud and have students take turns reading for the listeners in their pairs or groups.

ost-reading Activity: Use this activity to extend the fluency pre-reading activity. Discuss how Tomie dePaola wrote the story in lines instead of paragraphs. Ask how this affects the reading and fluidity of the story. Have students rewrite the paragraph on the Line by Line reproducible (page 85) using Tomie dePaola's style. Instruct students to "chunk" or group words by lines, in a way that "goes with" the reading. After stressing that there is no "right" answer, (since different readers will have different interpretations), have students compare notes. This activity can be used as a teaching tool on an overhead projector as you model the activity for students, or it can be done as a practice or assessment activity individually or in pairs.

Line by Line

fluency reproducible for

The Legend of the Indian Paintbrush

Name_____ Date_____

Rewrite the following paragraph on the lines below and on the back of this page, if necessary. Use Tomie dePaola's writing style of organizing the text by lines instead of paragraphs. "Chunk" the words according to the rhythm of how they should sound when you read them orally. Write them so readers will know how to read them.

    The small boy did not run and fight with the other warriors. His mother and father were worried, because he was so different from the other boys. The shaman of his tribe told him that he had a gift, and that this gift made him unique and special. One day the young boy saw a vision of a grandfather and a maiden who told him that he should paint the deeds of his People, as well as capture the colors of the sunset. Although it was very difficult, the young boy never gave up. One night, he went to a hillside and found in the ground all of the colors he needed. He painted a beautiful sunset and was always remembered by his People.

_____

_____

_____

_____

_____

_____

_____

_____

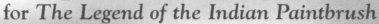

Comprehension Activities
for *The Legend of the Indian Paintbrush*

Pre-reading Activity: This activity helps students preview the literature and also make personal connections with it. Tell students that Little Gopher has a goal, but it is very difficult for him to achieve it. If necessary, talk about what goals are and how a person can achieve a goal. Ask students to predict what Little Gopher's goal is. Have students think about something that was hard for them to do, and write about it. Prompt students, "What is one thing you had a hard time doing? How did you feel when you were having difficulty with something? How did you achieve your goal? If you have not achieved your goal yet, what do you need to do in order to reach it?" Then, encourage students to see if their experiences and feelings are similar to those of Little Gopher's.

During-reading Activity: As students read the book, have them form opinions based on story evidence about Little Gopher. Review what an opinion is. Tell students that they will give opinions for this activity, but will have to convince you that their opinions are correct. For example, say, "My opinion is that this book is wonderful. My proof that it is a wonderful book is that it is entertaining, has beautiful illustrations, is an ABA Pick of the List book, and my students of past years have always enjoyed it." Tell students that they should form opinions about the book's main character, Little Gopher, and that they will have to find proof in the book to support their opinions of him. Model this first with a character from a well-known or previously read story. As an example, you might use Goldilocks by saying, "My opinion of the character Goldilocks is that she is disrespectful. As I look through the story, I can find proof to support my opinion. She went into someone's house without permission, and she tasted their food without asking." Before directing students to begin working, have each student fold a piece of paper in half vertically to form two columns. Have each student label the first column *Opinion* and the second column *Proof*. As students read the story, have them write their opinions about Little Gopher in the first column, and their proof from the story in the second column. You may want to model this or do it as a class activity while reading the book. For example, say, "So far, my opinion of Little Gopher is that he is artistic and creative. Let me write that in my first column. The proof from the story is that it says he 'was not without a gift of his own. . . he made toy warriors. . . and he loved to decorate smooth stones. . .' (*The Legend of the Indian Paintbrush*, page 3). I will write that in my second column to support, or prove, my opinion." Review students' answers as a whole class.

Post-reading Activity: Discuss how Little Gopher's name changed at the end. Ask students, "Why was his name changed? What did his first name symbolize? What did his new name mean?" Tell students to imagine that they could change their names to names like Little Gopher, based on achieving goals or making accomplishments. Have students create names for themselves beginning with "He-Who. . ." or "She-Who . . ." Brainstorm some possible ideas and discuss why they would be good names for certain individuals. Have students write their new names along with paragraphs explaining their choices on copies of the My Name Is . . . reproducible (page 87) and share them with their classmates.

My Name Is . . .
comprehension reproducible for
The Legend of the Indian Paintbrush

Name_____ Date_____

Think of a name you could give yourself that is similar to the new name Little Gopher receives. Write your new name on the paintbrush below. Then, explain why this would be a good name for you on the buckskin.

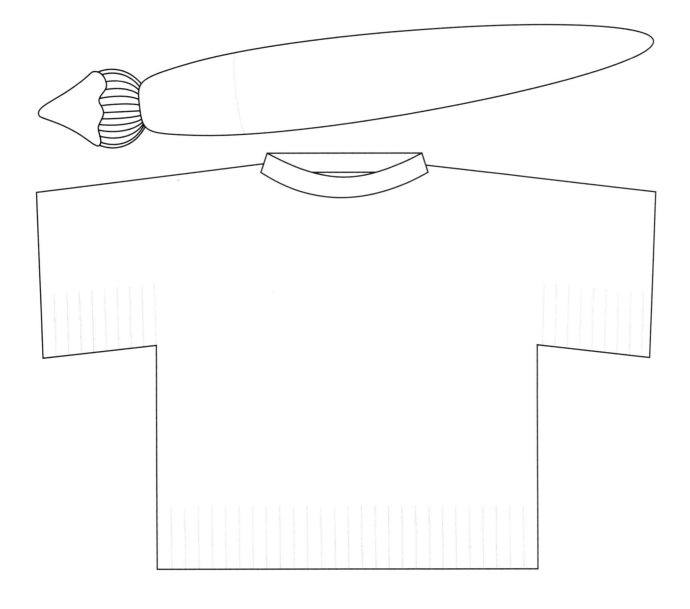

(Philomel, 1989)

Lon Po Po is the Chinese version of the fairy tale *Red-Riding Hood*. Students will recognize the *Red-Riding Hood* concept, but the story has enough differences to make it seem new. In this version, a mother leaves her three children at home for the night. A wolf appears, pretending to be their grandmother, but the three children work together to save themselves. The story has rich vocabulary and flowing dialogue.

Related books: *Cat and Rat: The Legend of the Chinese Zodiac* by Ed Young (Henry Holt & Company, 1998); *Little Red Riding Hood: A Newfangled Prairie Tale* by Lisa Campbell Ernst (Simon & Schuster, 1995); *Red Riding Hood* by James Marshall (Dutton, 1987); *Seven Blind Mice* by Ed Young (Philomel Books, 1992)

Phonemic Awareness Activities
for *Lon Po Po: A Red-Riding Hood Story from China*

Pre-reading Activity: Students will learn what *Lon Po Po* means from the vocabulary activities. Have students say the word *Po*. How many sounds do they hear? Identify the sounds (/p/, long /o/). Remind students that the smallest sound they hear in a word is called a *phoneme*. Call on students to isolate and count the number of phonemes in words you choose from the story. For example, say, "Latch." Have students repeat, then say, "Let's divide the word into phonemes: /l/, short /a/, /ch/. How many phonemes did you hear? (three)." See the post-reading activity for an extension.

During-reading Activity: Prior to the reading, make index cards with story words for students to separate into phonemes. Distribute the index cards. As you read the story aloud, have students hold up their cards when they hear their words. Pause when a student holds up a card, let him read the word, and have the class repeat it. Then, count the phonemes for that word and continue reading.

Post-reading Activity: Practice counting phonemes. Assign students to pairs or small groups. Give each pair a copy of the Counting Phonemes reproducible (page 89). Remind students that the children in *Lon Po Po* tricked the wolf with ginkgo nuts. Model using nuts to count the phonemes in the words on the list. Read the first word, reread it, and place a nut on a table for each phoneme. For example, for the word *who*, each pair will put down two nuts to represent /h/, /oo/). Read the word again and say how many phonemes it has. Tell students that if there are disagreements about how many phonemes are in words, they must work together to solve them.

phonemic awareness reproducible for

for *Lon Po Po: A Red-Riding Hood Story from China*

Name_____ Date_____

Work with a partner or your group to practice counting phonemes in words. Use a nut or other object to count each phoneme.

once   number of phonemes: _____

woman   number of phonemes: _____

who   number of phonemes: _____

three   number of phonemes: _____

children   number of phonemes: _____

old   number of phonemes: _____

wolf   number of phonemes: _____

dusk   number of phonemes: _____

grandmother   number of phonemes: _____

po   number of phonemes: _____

light   number of phonemes: _____

sweet   number of phonemes: _____

hemp   number of phonemes: _____

basket   number of phonemes: _____

hairy   number of phonemes: _____

visit   number of phonemes: _____

lon   number of phonemes: _____

ginkgo   number of phonemes: _____

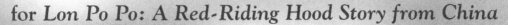

Phonics Activities
for *Lon Po Po: A Red-Riding Hood Story from China*

Pre-reading Activity: Tell students that they will be reading a story about a wolf who dresses up like a grandmother. Write the word *grandmother* on the board and circle the first two letters. Ask students to identify what sounds the letter g makes and what sound the letter r makes. Ask if they still make those sounds when they are put together (yes). Explain that when two consonants are put together but still make their separate sounds, it is called a *consonant blend*. Tell students that in the story the wolf pretends to be a grandmother, so they will pretend to be letters. Choose two students. Have one hold an index card with the consonant g and the other hold a card with the consonant r. Tell students to pretend to be the letters they are holding. Ask the "letter g" to stand alone and have the class make the hard /g/ sound. Repeat for the "letter r." Now, ask the two "letters" to stand close to each other (so close that they "blend" together). Then, have the class say the sounds. Repeat with other consonant blends (st, pr, tr, pl, cl, cr, str, br, dr, sp, fl, fr, bl, sl, sw, sm, sc, sk, gl, tw, scr, spr, sn, spl). Select one blend and ask students to help you list words that begin with that blend. Then, distribute the consonant cards to different groups so that each group can make at least one blend. For example, give one group the p, r, and t cards to form the tr and pr blends. Have each group think of and write at least three words with the blend(s), and share them with the class.

During-reading Activity: Write the words *Lon Po Po* on the board and underline the letter o in each word. Ask students what sound the letter o makes and have students sound out the words. Point out that the letter o makes the short /o/ sound in *Lon* and the long /o/ sound in *Po*. Next, write *wolf* and *grandmother* on the board, and underline the letter o in each. Ask which word makes the short /o/ sound and which makes the long /o/ sound. Students will quickly realize that neither o makes a typical sound. The o in *wolf* makes the same sound as /oo/ in *wool*. The o in *grandmother* makes the same short /u/ sound as in *umbrella*. As students read the book, or as you read it aloud, have them list words that contain the letter o on copies of the Sounds Like O reproducible (page 91). Then, instruct them to mark out words with vowel teams, leaving words with o's between consonants. Finally, have each student use the key to code different sounds of the letter o.

Post-reading Activity: Tell students that when the letter r follows a vowel, the vowel no longer makes a long or short sound. Instead it makes the "bossy r" (r-controlled) sound like at the end of the word *grandmother*. Write *grandmother* on the board and underline the two letters creating the bossy r sound. Tell students that this is called the bossy r sound because the r "bosses" the vowel to change its sound to sound more like the r. Divide students into groups or pairs and challenge them to find as many bossy r-words as they can in the story. Have each group title a sheet of paper *Bossy R* and divide it into five vertical columns labeled *ar/er/ir/or/ur*. Have each group record all of the bossy-r words from the story on the sheet of paper. Review the book as a class, confirm bossy-r words, and announce the winning group as the "Bosses of the Bossy R's."

Sounds Like O

phonics reproducible for

Lon Po Po: A Red-Riding Hood Story from China

Name_____ Date_____

On the lines below, write all of the words you find with the letter o. Do not write the same word twice. Then, mark out all of the words in which o appears next to another vowel, or next to the letter y. Use the back of the page if necessary.

_____   _____   _____

_____   _____   _____

_____   _____   _____

_____   _____   _____

_____   _____   _____

_____   _____   _____

_____   _____   _____

_____   _____   _____

_____   _____   _____

_____   _____   _____

_____   _____   _____

_____   _____   _____

_____   _____   _____

_____   _____   _____

Use this key to code the different sounds of o. Underline all of the short /o/ words, such as *Lon*, with red. Circle all of the long /o/ words, such as *Po*, with blue. Draw a black box around each word with the short /u/ sound, like *grandmother*. Draw a squiggly blue line under each word that has a sound like oo in *wolf*. Use a highlighter to mark all of the words that have an r-controlled o sound, like *or*. If you find other sounds that o makes, make up a color-code for them, too.

Vocabulary Activities
for *Lon Po Po: A Red-Riding Hood Story from China*

Pre-reading Activity: Tell students that they will be reading a story about a wolf who pretends to be a grandmother. Write the word *grandmother* on the board and ask students to identify the two words that make up the word (*grand* and *mother*). Discuss the possibilities of why this is the name for such a person. What does the word *grand* mean? What would a grand person be like? Tell students that when two words are put together to make one new word, it is called a *compound word*. Brainstorm other compound words and write them on the board. Tell students to listen for other compound words in the story (*birthday, sunset, nearby, forever, yourself, outside*).

During-reading Activity: Explain that in the book *Lon Po Po*, the author has included some "noise words" to help readers "hear" the story better. Explain what *onomatopoeia* means. Tell students that they must listen for "noise words" as you read the story. Direct students to signal that they have heard a "noise word" by covering their ears with their hands in an exaggerated way. Give them an opportunity to practice this as you say the words *meow, crash,* and *boom*. After you have read the story aloud and students have identified the noise words (*bang bang, hei yo*), tell them that when an author uses noise words it is called *onomatopoeia*. Discuss other examples of onomatopoeia such as *drip, plop, screech,* etc. Tell students that you will read the story again, but this time they will add onomatopoeia. For example, have students say "crash" when the wolf falls in the basket or "whish" when the candle is blown out.

Post-reading Activity: Remind students that many times they will encounter unfamiliar or confusing words while reading. Discuss what strategies and resources they can use when this occurs (dictionary, context clues, ask someone, skip it, sound it out, etc.). Explain that good readers use different strategies for different situations. List the following story words on the board: *Lon Po Po, cunning, awl, ginkgo, hemp*. Have students use copies of the New Word Watch reproducible (page 93) as guides to figure out the words' meanings. After students are finished working with the words, discuss each word and the steps students used to figure out its meaning. Point out that it is not necessary to look up some words, such as *Po Po*, in the dictionary because using the story and common sense makes the definitions understandable. Point out that it doesn't matter what the precise definition is for some words, as long as the reader has a general understanding, such as with *ginkgo* and *hemp*. Encourage students to keep the reproducibles for future reference and use them during independent reading times.

New Word Watch

vocabulary reproducible for

Lon Po Po: A Red-Riding Hood Story from China

Name_____ Date_____

When you are reading and come to an unfamiliar word, you can try many strategies to help you figure out the word's meaning. Use story words that your teacher assigns. On a separate sheet of paper, complete the steps below to figure out each word's meaning. After you have practiced doing this on paper a few times, you should be able to follow the steps in your head!

Reread the unfamiliar word.

Copy the sentence from the text that contains the word.

Are there any clues in the sentence that might help you guess the meaning of the word? If so, what are they? Write them below the sentence.

Reread the sentences surrounding the sentence that the unknown word is in. Are there any clues in these sentences? Think about what is happening in the story. What word might make sense here?

Try plugging in a known word where the unknown word is. Rewrite the sentence and substitute a word that might make sense in place of the unfamiliar word.

If you still can't figure out the word's meaning, ask yourself: Is it important that I know this word? If I don't know the word, will it affect my overall comprehension of the story? If not, then skip it and keep reading. Forget about the unfamiliar word!

If not knowing the word does affect your comprehension, then use a dictionary. Look up the word, and read all of the definitions to see which one would make the most sense in this context.

Fluency Activities
for *Lon Po Po: A Red-Riding Hood Story from China*

Pre-reading Activity: Explain that when a reader reads aloud he must sound fluent. Tell students that fluency is an important part of reading because not only do readers sound "better" when they read fluently, but fluency helps listeners and readers understand the story. One way fluency helps with understanding is that readers can "see" and "hear" the characters better if dialogue and action are read in a realistic way. Tell students that in the story *Lon Po Po*, there are many parts where the characters talk to each other. This is called *dialogue*. Dialogue should sound the way the characters would sound in real life during a similar situation. Tell students that in *Lon Po Po*, the main characters are confused and in danger. Ask students how they might sound if they were confused and in danger. Explain that the main characters get out of danger by tricking another character. Ask students to role-play how they would sound if they were saying something to someone to trick them. Then, tell students to listen to you read to evaluate whether you are reading fluently and sounding like people would in real life.

During-reading Activity: Reread the story and have students echo read the dialogue parts after you. Tell students to pay particular attention to your expression. Does each character sound afraid? Confused? Persuasive? Encourage them to imitate your expressions. As you read the story and students echo the dialogue parts, praise students and comment on the expression, tonality, and feeling in their voices.

Post-reading Activity: Ask students why they think the wolf believed the girls' trick. Discuss how a person must sound when she is trying to convince someone to do something. Role-play some possible scenarios such as a time a student tried to convince her parents to raise her allowance or when she tried to get someone to believe that she really had not done something. Pair students and have each pair write a short scene in which one character tries to trick or persuade the other character, the way the wolf tried to trick the girls and the girls tricked the wolf. Give them time to practice reading their lines. Tell them to focus on reading the lines fluently and with expression—the way a person would use his voice when attempting to persuade someone. Then, have pairs read their scenes to the class. Have the class rate each student's fluency with copies of the You Can't Fool Me! reproducible (page 95).

First-Rate Reading™ Grade 3 • CD-0071 • © Carson-Dellosa

You Can't Fool Me!

fluency reproducible for

Lon Po Po: A Red-Riding Hood Story from China

Name_____ Date_____

Use this sheet to rate your classmates' scenes. Write each reader's name on a line. Then, circle 1, 2, or 3 to rate his or her fluency.

1 = The reader read fluently, had good expression, sounded natural, and sounded like a real person.
2 = The reader read somewhat fluently, but needs more practice.
3 = The reader did not read fluently, and did not sound like a real person talking.

Reader's Name	Fluency Score			Comments
_____	1	2	3	_____
_____	1	2	3	_____
_____	1	2	3	_____
_____	1	2	3	_____
_____	1	2	3	_____
_____	1	2	3	_____
_____	1	2	3	_____
_____	1	2	3	_____
_____	1	2	3	_____
_____	1	2	3	_____
_____	1	2	3	_____
_____	1	2	3	_____

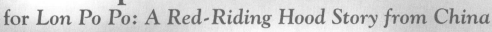

Comprehension Activities
for *Lon Po Po: A Red-Riding Hood Story from China*

Pre-reading Activity: Tell students that the story *Lon Po Po* is the Chinese version of *Red-Riding Hood*. Have each student fold a piece of paper in half vertically to make two columns, and label one column *Red-Riding Hood* and the other *Lon Po Po*. Have each student brainstorm and list everything she knows about *Red-Riding Hood* in the first column. Instruct her to leave the second column blank for now. Then, have the student look at the book cover, preview some of the pages, and predict what will be the same and what will be different between this version and the traditional *Red-Riding Hood*. Have each student list at least one predicted difference and one predicted similarity on the back of her paper. Ask a few students to share their predictions. Tell students to keep their knowledge of *Red-Riding Hood* and their predictions in mind while reading.

During-reading Activity: Read the story aloud and have students jot down notes under the second columns they filled out in the pre-reading activity (above). Instruct them to write things that are different between the traditional *Red-Riding Hood* and *Lon Po Po*. Pause after you read the first page to demonstrate how to write notes and think aloud. As you write, say, "I already see that in this version there are three children, instead of one like there is in *Red-Riding Hood*. So, I'm going to write that in my *Lon Po Po* column." Write *three children* on the board. "I also see that in this story the mother is the one who leaves to visit the grandmother instead of the children. I'll note that, too." Write *The mother leaves to visit Grandmother*. After reading the story, create a class chart from students' individual charts and discuss the two versions. Tell students that what they did required them to think as they read, and that good readers always think as they read, which is called *active reading*.

Post-reading Activity: Tell students that the wolf probably did not fool the children because he unintentionally gave clues about his identity during the story. Have students find the clues that might have made the children suspicious and list them on copies of the Wolf in Grandmother's Clothing reproducible (page 97). Then, have them write and illustrate what they would have done if they were the children in the story. Display the work on a bulletin board titled "You Can't Fool Us!"

Wolf in Grandmother's Clothing

comprehension reproducible for

Lon Po Po: A Red-Riding Hood Story from China

Name_____ Date_____

There are different clues in the story that tell the children that a wolf has come to visit. Some of these clues are visual. (They can be seen.) Some of these clues are auditory. (They can be heard.) And, some are tactile. (They can be felt.) As you read the story, list the different clues under the types of clues that they are. On the back of this paper, write what you would have done if the wolf tried to trick you.

Visual clues: _____

_____

_____

_____

_____

Auditory clues: _____

_____

_____

_____

_____

Tactile clues: _____

_____

_____

_____

_____

 _____

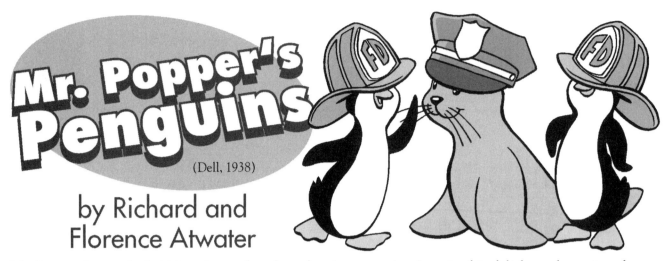

Mr. Popper's Penguins

(Dell, 1938)

by Richard and Florence Atwater

Mr. Popper dreamed of visiting the south pole and seeing penguins. Imagine his delight and surprise when he receives a penguin from the great Admiral Drake! The Popper family becomes quite fond of the new pet, but they never would have guessed that they would end up with a whole family of trained show penguins!

Related books: *The Cricket in Times Square* by George Selden (Random House, 1970); *The Mouse and the Motorcycle* by Beverly Cleary (HarperTrophy, 1990); *Owls in the Family* by Farley Mowat (Laureleaf, 1996); *Pinky Pye* by Eleanor Estes (Turtleback Books, 2000)

Phonemic Awareness Activities
for *Mr. Popper's Penguins*

Pre-reading Activity: Read the title to students and ask what phoneme they hear repeatedly (/p/). Challenge students to say the title five times fast. Tell students that when they hear the same initial sound several times it is called *alliteration*. Alliteration makes it difficult to say things repeatedly and quickly—words become tongue twisters. Ask students to say this as well: *Mr. Popper's penguins pranced proudly on the prairie.* Then, brainstorm more /p/ words to add to the title to create more /p/ tongue twisters. Challenge students to think of words that contain more than one /p/ sound such as *puppy, popcorn, popping, porcupine,* etc.

During-reading Activity: The penguins in this book "talk" to the Poppers. As you read, pause whenever the penguins speak, and ask students to isolate each grapheme and sound it out. Then, have them put the phonemes together to make the penguins' sounds. Review vowel digraph aw, basic consonant and vowel phonemes, qu, and hard /g/. Penguin "words" to look for are *ork, gook, gork, orrrrh, gaw,* and *quork.*

Post-reading Activity: This activity enables students to practice sorting words according to different phonemes. Give each student a copy of the Sorting Phonemes reproducible (page 99). Read the words together to ensure students know how to pronounce each word and discuss how each word relates to the story. Instruct students to cut out the word cards, then sort the words according to as many phonemic patterns as they can find. If students have difficulty finding phonemic patterns, guide them in several different ways. For example, instruct them to sort words according to beginning, medial, or initial phonemes. Other categories for sorting include words that contain silent letters, r-controlled vowels, number of syllables, long/short vowel sounds, vowel digraphs, etc. This activity can be varied to review previous phonemic lessons, introduce new ones, and/or assess students' levels.

Sorting Phonemes

phonemic awareness reproducible for

Mr. Popper's Penguins

Name _____ Date _____

Cut out the word cards. When your teacher tells you to, sort the words into phonemic categories.

mister	Popper	penguins	Antarctic
poles	untidy	south	north
pets	Admiral	cool	perform
flippers	trouble	Captain	Cook
children	housekeeper	expedition	regretted
Greta	paint	ice	jail

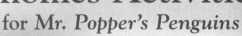 

Pre-reading Activity: Prior to this activity, program index cards with the following syllables: *ap, ple, bet, ter, but, ter, dad, dy, dol, lar, fol, low, hap, pen, hol, low, lad, der, pret, ty, pup, py, sum, mer, yel, low, zip, per.* Write the book title on the board and have students read it. Ask them to count the number of syllables in each word. Take a moment to discuss how *Mr.* has two syllables because it is an abbreviation for the word *mister.* Ask a student to draw lines on the board between syllables for the rest of the words. Have students notice that the word *Popper* should be divided between the p's. Tell students that when a word has more than one syllable and a double consonant, it is always divided between those two consonants. Pass out the syllable cards at random. Have each student walk around the room looking for his "other half." Remind students that the words are divided between double consonants, so they should look for matching ending and initial consonants in their syllables. Make the game more exciting by awarding pairs who find each other within a given time limit, or repeat the activity by shuffling the cards.

During-reading Activity: While reading chapter 1, stop to discuss what Mr. Popper's biggest regret was (never seeing the poles). Have students find the sentences that support this answer in the text. Ask students to notice how the word *regret* changes when adding the suffix ed. Tell students that when a base word ends with a short vowel followed by a consonant, the final consonant is doubled before adding the suffix. Tell students that this rule applies to adding ing as well. Challenge them to find an example of this on the next page of the text: "'Well, my love,'" he said, setting down his buckets. . ." (*Mr. Popper's Penguins*, page 7). As students proceed through the reading, encourage students to look for more examples. Then, have students complete the Double Consonant reproducible (page 101) after reading the chapter.

Post-reading Activity: Ask students what sound they hear and what letter they see most in the book. They should notice that the letter p appears quite often, not just in the title, but in the book as well. The Poppers live on Proudfoot Avenue, Mr. Popper is a painter and wallpaperer, the children call him Papa, the penguins perform and come from the south pole, etc. Assign students to 13 pairs or small groups and give each a chapter. (You may also have students do this individually.) Let groups take turns at a center searching their chapters for words that contain the letter p. Instruct each group to write each word on an index card or piece of sentence strip. Then, have a student in each group highlight the letter p in each word. Words with more than one p should have all of the p's highlighted. Reward all of the groups with prizes that begin with the letter p but give the largest prize to the group that finds the most words. Also reward the groups with the longest word, shortest word, etc. Post the words on a bulletin board titled "Phonics Starts with P!"

Double Consonant

phonics reproducible for
Mr. Popper's Penguins

Name_____ Date_____

Mr. Popper's penguins have words from the book written on their bellies. Match the penguins outside of the box with the penguins inside of the box by connecting each base word to its correctly spelled suffix.

ted   ging   ping   ting   red   ting

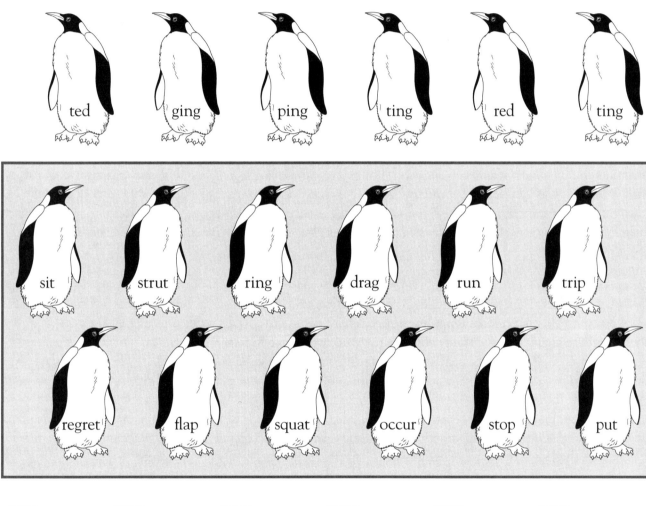

sit   strut   ring   drag   run   trip

regret   flap   squat   occur   stop   put

ting   ing   ped   ning   ted   ping

Vocabulary Activities
for *Mr. Popper's Penguins*

Pre-reading Activity: Because this book uses many old-fashioned words, it is important that students know how to decipher their meanings without going to dictionaries every time. Tell students that because the book was originally published in 1938, much of the language may seem "fancy" or old-fashioned to them. The Poppers speak very properly and use words and phrases that are uncommon today such as *quite pleased, prospect, chap, untidy*, etc. Tell students that although dictionaries are important and very useful, it is not always practical (or enjoyable) to stop to look up words. This is especially the case in a books such as *Mr. Popper's Penguins*, where the words are not necessarily difficult to figure out. On the board, write phrases and sentences from the book which contain words such as *spattered, whiskers, untidy, spectacles, quite pleased, prospect, disagreeable, cross*, etc. Read the sentences with students and discuss some of the old-fashioned words. Then, guide students toward figuring out what the sentences mean and have students help you rewrite them in more contemporary language. For example, say, "Look at the last sentence. What do you think *disagreeable* means? Think about what it means when someone agrees. What do you suppose it means to disagree? Then, the phrase on page 11, '. . . but she sometimes got rather cross when she was worried about money.' gives us a clue, too. How can we rewrite this sentence using more modern, common language? What are they saying about Mrs. Popper?" (Help students realize that the author means that Mrs. Popper was a nice woman, but sometimes she got mad when she was worried about money.)

During-reading Activity: As students proceed through the book, have them "collect" words for a class vocabulary list. If students are reading independently, instruct them to write interesting words on sticky notes, and use them to mark the pages on which the words are found. After the day's reading is complete, allow students to share some of the words and add them to the class vocabulary list. Then, have students use dictionaries and the words' sentences to define the words. If students are reading together as a class, instruct them to raise their hands when they come to words they do not know or understand. Then, pause as a class to discuss and define each word. The accumulated list of vocabulary words can be used for spelling and/or definition tests, practice with alphabetizing, or to create a word wall. Some possible words to use from the book are *untidy, absentminded, regretted, curiosity, pompous, strut*, etc.

Post-reading Activity: After finishing the book, have each student use the vocabulary words studied to write a newspaper article about Mr. Popper's Penguins. Select new vocabulary words or use words collected from the during-reading activity (above). Have students use the Front Page News reproducible (page 103) as a guide to create their newspaper articles. Have students refer to actual newspaper articles prior to writing in order to make their articles more authentic.

Front Page News
vocabulary reproducible for
Mr. Popper's Penguins

Name_____ Date_____

Pretend you are a newspaper reporter covering the famous Popper's Penguins. Write an article for the front page of the newspaper using as many of the vocabulary words as possible.

New bridge
open to
traffic
Section B

News Time

Football
draft
results
Section C

continued page 3

Local student wins state spelling bee

Fluency Activities
for *Mr. Popper's Penguins*

Pre-reading Activity: Reveal to students that this book was first published in 1938. Discuss how the publication date might affect the story's language, characters, setting, etc. Ask students if they think the characters would speak the same way we do now. (Bring up issues like slang, idiomatic speech, etc.) Tell students that the language in this book is a little different from some other books they might have read. (Good comparisons are: *Amber Brown Is Not a Crayon* by Paula Danziger, *Junie B. Jones and the Stupid Smelly Bus* by Barbara Park, and *Judy Moody* by Megan McDonald.) This is because the characters do not use slang or child-like talk. Instead, they speak very properly and use old-fashioned words. Ask students if they think this will affect the way a reader sounds while reading the book aloud. Consider role-playing how an older person in 1938 might sound while speaking versus a how a younger person would sound today. Tell students to listen for the differences in your voice, intonations, and expressions when you read aloud.

During-reading Activity: The dialogue and language of this book lend themselves to practicing fluency. There are several scenes in which students can practice oral reading. For example, the scene in chapter 6 when the policeman comes to the door is a perfect opportunity to do echo reading because of the dialogue and different emotional reactions of the characters. Point out to students how the policeman is somewhat afraid and nervous, as well as very confused, while Bill and Janie are amused and very matter-of-fact. Read this scene using echo reading so that students have an opportunity to mimic your very expressive and fluent reading of the dialogue. Other scenes which are ideal for echo reading are when Mr. Popper inquires about getting a license for the penguin (chapter 6), the barber shop scene in chapter 9, the scene in the Minneapolis theater with the opera singer (chapter 17), the scene in which Mr. Popper gets arrested (chapter 18), and when Mr. Popper decides to leave on the expedition (chapter 18).

Post-reading Activity: This activity will give students an opportunity to practice fluency, but will also help train them to identify characteristics of fluent readers. Tell students that they will pretend to be the theater managers where Mr. Popper's penguins performed. Instruct students to write short skits in which they will introduce the penguins to the audience prior to their performance. They should include details such as where the penguins come from, what tricks they will perform, their names, and the songs being used. Discuss how an announcer might sound in such a situation. Would he read his introduction in a shy, quiet voice? Would he stumble over words? Or, would he be clear, loud, and excited in order to get the audience enthused? After students write their introductions, have them rehearse reading them aloud several times. Then, have students take turns presenting their introductions to the class. Classmates should evaluate the announcers using copies of the Now Showing reproducible (page 105).

Now Showing
fluency reproducible for
Mr. Popper's Penguins

Name_____ Date_____

Listen as your classmates "announce" Popper's Penguins for the theater audience. Evaluate their fluency below. Write "yes" or "no" in the blanks.

Announcer's name _____
Was the announcer's voice loud and clear? _____
Did the announcer read all of the words smoothly and naturally? _____
Was the announcer's voice excited and expressive? _____
From what the announcer said, what kind of show do you expect to see and how do you feel about it? _____

_____

_____

Announcer's name _____
Was the announcer's voice loud and clear? _____
Did the announcer read all of the words smoothly and naturally? _____
Was the announcer's voice excited and expressive? _____
From what the announcer said, what kind of show do you expect to see and how do you feel about it? _____

_____

_____

Announcer's name _____
Was the announcer's voice loud and clear? _____
Did the announcer read all of the words smoothly and naturally? _____
Was the announcer's voice excited and expressive? _____
From what the announcer said, what kind of show do you expect to see and how do you feel about it? _____

_____

_____

Comprehension Activities
for *Mr. Popper's Penguins*

Pre-reading Activity: This is an excellent book to practice predicting because the events are, in fact, so unpredictable. Present students with the title and cover and have each student write a one-sentence prediction based on that information. Then, read the blurb on the back and have each student write another, more specific prediction. Next, have each student read the chapter titles and write a final, even more specific prediction for the book. Let students share predictions and discuss how each time they were able to make more detailed and accurate predictions because they could preview more information. Revisit the predictions during and after reading.

During-reading Activity: Much of what students are asked to do in the area of comprehension is to answer questions about information they have read. Use the Comprehension Questions reproducible (page 107) to assess comprehension as students read the book. Then, give the activity a twist. Explain the difference between lower-order and higher-order questions. A lower-order question asks for information about facts that can be found directly in the reading. For example, lower-order questions about *Mr. Popper's Penguins* might be, "What was the first penguin's name? Where did he live?" A higher-order question requires critical thinking. For example, "Was Mrs. Popper happy about having penguins as pets? Why do you think so?" As students finish reading each chapter, have them write questions about the chapter, then indicate whether the questions are lower-order or higher-order. Let students trade questions and answer them.

Post-reading Activity: Have students write a "chapter 21." Tell them to brainstorm what they think will happen next in the book: how long Mr. Popper will be gone, what he will do and see in his expedition, how the penguins will fare, how Mrs. Popper and the children will get along without him, etc. Have each student write what she thinks would have happened in chapter 21. Then, create a class mural of Mr. Popper on his expedition. Have students illustrate and color the final scene on a large sheet of white bulletin board paper. Let students use white chalk, cotton, and silver glitter to add snow. Then, attach the "chapter 21's" to the mural. Display them in the classroom or a hallway.

Comprehension Questions
comprehension reproducible for
Mr. Popper's Penguins

Name_____ Date_____

After reading each group of chapters, answer the following questions on a separate sheet of paper. Remember to go back to the story to search for evidence and clues.

Chapters 1-4
1. What kind of personality does Mrs. Popper have? Find evidence in the story to support your answer.

2. How do you think Mr. Popper feels about Mrs. Popper? Find evidence in the story to support your answer.

3. List three things that have happened so far that are realistic. List three things that have happened that are fantasy.

Chapters 5-11
1. What are some of the "troubles" the Poppers have had due to the penguins?

2. Retell the main events in the story so far.

3. How do you think Mrs. Popper feels about having penguins in the house? Find details from the story to support your answer.

Chapters 12-17
1. Do you think it is a good idea to let the penguins perform? Why or why not?

2. Why do you think the penguins are "growing irritable"?

Chapters 18-20
1. Mr. Popper decided to let the penguins go to the north pole even though he gave up a lot of money from the movie producers. Why do you think he did that? What does this decision say about Mr. Popper?

2. How do you feel about the ending?

Ramona Quimby, Age 8

by Beverly Cleary

(William Morrow
& Co., 1981)

Ramona is excited about third grade, until a boy takes her new eraser and her new sandals squeak in front of the class. Things get worse; she cracks a raw egg on her head, overhears her teacher call her a "nuisance," and throws up in class. The things that happen to Ramona are as current now as when Beverly Cleary invented her.

Related books by Beverly Cleary: *Beezus and Ramona* (HarperTrophy, 1993); *Ramona and Her Father* (HarperTrophy, 1999); *Ramona and Her Mother* (HarperTrophy, 1990); *Ramona Forever* (HarperTrophy, 1995); *Ramona the Brave* (HarperTrophy, 1995); *Ramona the Pest* (HarperTrophy, 1996)

Phonemic Awareness Activities
for *Ramona Quimby, Age 8*

Pre-reading Activity: Allow students to preview the chapter titles. Write "The Quimbys' Quarrel" (chapter 4's title) on the board. Ask what students notice about these words (the qu pattern). Tell them that q is almost always followed by u. Q and u together usually make the /kw/ sound. Ask students to say the difference between the initial sound in *Quimby* and in *kid*. (One is /kw/; the other is /k/.) Explain that sometimes the letters qu also make the /k/ sound (usually when the qu is at the end of a syllable or word). Write *technique, clique, mosquito*, and *unique* on the board. Have students divide these words into syllables by clapping, counting, or putting their fingers under their chins. Then, write *liquid, equal, quick*, and *quiet* on the board. Have students read the words and count the syllables.

During-reading Activity: In chapter 2, pause when Bruce, Ramona, and Willa Jean play dress-up and sing "Mr. Frog Would A-wooing Go." Have students sound out the "word" *hm-m* from the song and tell if it is a "real" word. Explain that this is the way the author wrote the humming sound that the characters made. Ask students when an author might write the sound *uh-uh*. (When a person says "no.") Repeat for other "sounds" such as *mm-hmm* (yes). Ask students to make other sounds with meanings and decide what letters could represent those sounds. Break apart the "words" carefully so students can hear each phoneme in isolation. Write the "words."

Post-reading Activity: Have students return to chapter 4. How did Beezus know she was eating tongue? (She felt the rough surface.) Write *rough* on the board. Have students repeat it and identify the phonemes (/r/, short /u/, /f/). Have students identify which grapheme(s) represents each phoneme (/r/ = r; short /u/ = ou; /f/ = gh). Explain that gh usually represents three different sounds: hard /g/ as in *ghost*, silent as in *bright*, and /f/ as in *rough*. Copy the Gh Word Cards reproducible (page 109). Have students cut out the word cards, then work to identify the gh's as making the /f/ sound, hard /g/ sound, or no sound.

Name_____ Date_____

Cut apart the word cards. Work with a partner to sort the word cards into three categories: gh makes the /f/ sound, /gh/ makes the hard /g/ sound, and gh makes no sound (is silent).

right	tough	high
laughed	cough	daughters
sighed	spaghetti	enough
through	sight	thought
ghastly	ought	eight

Phonics Activities
for *Ramona Quimby, Age 8*

Pre-reading Activity: Write the title on the board. Ask if anyone can spell the number word for 8. Have a volunteer write the word *eight* on the board. Point out that the letters ght make the /t/ sound because the g and h are silent. Brainstorm a list of other words that end in ght such as *ought, fright, flight, sight, caught*, etc. Include these words on a spelling list or word wall. You may want to point out the gh words on the Gh Word Cards reproducible (page 109).

During-reading Activity: Tell students that although many consonants represent their consonant sounds most of the time, sometimes consonants can be silent, too. For example, the letter l usually makes the /l/ sound, but sometimes it is silent such as in the word *yolk*. (Note that some regional dialects do pronounce the l.) Point this out to students when reading the part where Ramona breaks an egg over her head in chapter 3, "The Hard-boiled Egg Fad." Give students pre-cut white circles ("fried eggs") and tell them that they will search for other words containing silent consonants while they read this chapter. When a student finds a word with a silent consonant, have her write the word on an "egg" and highlight the silent letter(s) with yellow. Some words to look for in the chapter are *eight, brought, wouldn't, could, who, wrist, typewriter, right, numb*, and *dumb*.

Post-reading Activity: Use *Ramona Quimby, Age 8* to review how to alphabetize words. Provide example words from each chapter that begin with the same first, second, and third letters. For example, possible words to use in chapter 1 are *stomach, started, study, stopped*, etc. Remind students that the first letter is often not the only one they need to look at in order to alphabetize words. Then, use the Alphabetical Order reproducible (page 111) to provide students with an opportunity to practice alphabetizing.

Alphabetical Order
phonics reproducible for
Ramona Quimby, Age 8

Name_____ Date_____

Part 1: Reread the chapter titles below. Number them according to alphabetical order. Remember to look at the beginning letters of the second words if necessary. Remember, if the first word is *a, and,* or *the,* use the second word to alphabetize the titles.

_____ The First Day of School
_____ At Howie's House
_____ The Hard-boiled Egg
_____ The Quimbys' Quarrel
_____ The Extra-good Sunday
_____ Supernuisance
_____ The Patient
_____ Ramona's Book Report
_____ Rainy Sunday

Part 2: Rewrite the following story words in alphabetical order on the blank lines: Ramona, Howie, Beezus, egg, nuisance, Mrs. Kemp, Yard Ape, throw up, tongue, commercial, Sunday

_____

_____

_____

_____

Part 3: Select ONE word from EACH chapter. Write the words in the first set of numbered blanks. Then, rewrite them in alphabetical order.

1._____   6._____   1._____   6._____
2._____   7._____   2._____   7._____
3._____   8._____   3._____   8._____
4._____   9._____   4._____   9._____
5._____   5._____

Vocabulary Activities
for *Ramona Quimby, Age 8*

Pre-reading Activity: The word *nuisance* is critical to students' understanding of *Ramona Quimby, Age 8*. Much of the story's plot revolves around Ramona believing that her teacher thinks she is a nuisance. Tell students that in chapter 3, the main character, Ramona, overhears her teacher talking about her in the office. The teacher apparently calls Ramona a "nuisance." This makes Ramona feel terrible, and she decides that her teacher doesn't like her. Have students guess what a *nuisance* is and write their responses on the board. If students have an idea of the word's definition, encourage them to use it in sentences. If not, have a student look it up in a dictionary, and write the definition on the board. Once students understand the word's definition, have each write the definition of the word (either from the class discussion or dictionary), write another word that means about the same thing, write a sentence using the word, write a word or phrase that means the opposite of a person who is a nuisance, and illustrate or write a short story about someone being a nuisance.

During-reading Activity: While reading chapter 3, pause when Mrs. Whaley compliments Ramona's fruit-fly larvae label: "'That's a really neat label, Ramona,' said Mrs. Whaley. Ramona understood that her teacher did not mean tidy when she said 'neat,' but extra good." (*Ramona Quimby, Age 8*, page 58). Discuss how Ramona knew which *neat* Mrs. Whaley meant. Ask students to think of sentences using *neat* as in *tidy*. Tell students that some words, like *neat*, have multiple meanings. Continue reading and pause again when Ramona cracks a raw egg on her head: "She tried to brush the yellow yolk and slithery white out of her hair and away from her face. . ." (*Ramona Quimby, Age 8*, page 61). Ask students if the word *brush* in this sentence means a tool a person uses to fix hair or to wipe. Tell students that *brush* is another example of a word with multiple meanings. Use the Multiple Meanings reproducible (page 113) to decide the definitions for other story words with multiple meanings. Have each student read a sentence and look up the underlined word in a dictionary. Then, instruct her to choose the right meaning for that particular sentence and write it on the blank line. Note that students may need to look up root words if the words have suffixes or are in different tenses.

Post-reading Activity: Reread the part in chapter 2 when Ramona is happily doing her Sustained Silent Reading: "How peaceful it was to be left alone in school. . . .She was not expected to write lists of words she did not know, so she could figure them out by skipping and guessing." (*Ramona Quimby, Age 8*, page 41). Discuss what Ramona means by "skipping and guessing." Ask students how they feel about writing lists of words they don't know. Ask students if they ever "skip and guess." Tell students that although writing words they don't know as they read is one way to learn new words, there are other ways, too. As Ramona says, the reader can simply skip a word or guess its meaning. This can be done in a few different ways. One way is for the reader to skip the unknown word, read on, and then go back to the word to guess its meaning. Or, the reader can immediately guess what word might fit in place of the unknown word. A reader can also use other clues to help him guess, such as the first letter of the word. Finally, a reader can guess what a word means by asking himself what would make sense there. Demonstrate these reading strategies with some of the sentences from the chapter. Encourage students to do as Ramona does and "skip and guess" unknown words as they encounter them throughout their reading.

Multiple Meanings

vocabulary reproducible for
Ramona Quimby, Age 8

Name_____ Date_____

Read the story sentences below. Look up each underlined word in a dictionary and select the definition that means the same thing as the word in the sentence. Then, write the dictionary definition on the line. You may need to look up the root word in some words.

1. "<u>Drop</u> everything and read." (page 41)_____

_____

2. "The boys, of course, <u>paid</u> no attention." (page 31) _____

_____

3. "She <u>saw</u> some people she had known at her old school." (page 31) _____

_____

4. "Presents of any <u>kind</u> had been scarce while the family tried to save money." (page 17)

_____

5. "She saw her pink eraser <u>fly</u> back into Danny's hands." (page 29) _____

_____

6. "Ramona did not <u>mean</u> to break an egg in her hair." (pages 68-69) _____

_____

7. "Willa Jean <u>stamped</u> her foot." (page 49)_____

_____

8. "Here are those tests I was supposed to <u>hand</u> in yesterday." (page 67)_____

_____

Fluency Activities

for *Ramona Quimby, Age 8*

Pre-reading Activity: Read the blurb on the back cover aloud. Encourage students to follow along and notice your voice intonations, pauses, and expression. Ask students what the purpose of a book blurb is (to inform the reader and sell the book). Ask what students think the blurb should sound like when it is read aloud. If the publisher wants people to purchase the book, should the blurb be read in a cheerful tone? Should it be read quickly or slowly? Then, ask how the blurb on the back of a dictionary would sound. Read one if it is available. Ask why it would sound different from a children's fiction book. Then, reread the blurb from *Ramona Quimby, Age 8*, this time having students follow along chorally. Finally, have students take turns reading the blurb to each other in pairs.

During-reading Activity: Pause after reading chapter 8 and review Ramona's book report presentation. Discuss what made her presentation a success and how she could have improved. Have students find proof in the story for each point such as ". . .said Ramona in a loud clear voice. . ." and "She could not help interrupting herself. . ." Have students practice their fluency by writing and presenting their own commercials. The commercials can simply sell products, such as those on television, or can be book reports, such as the one Ramona did. Consider letting students make masks like the characters in the book did. Give students plenty of time to rehearse their scripts. Remind them to speak loudly and clearly, be comfortable enough to not stumble on words, be expressive, and pause when appropriate.

Post-reading Activity: Ramona learned that some parts of third grade were good while some parts were not so good. Discuss some of the great things about third grade (when Mrs. Whaley said her label was "neat," when Yard Ape was nice, etc.) and some of the not-so-great things (when she broke the egg on her head, when Yard Ape took her eraser, etc.). Have students brainstorm some things they like and dislike about third grade. Then, have students complete the What I Like about School reproducible (page 115). Instruct students to practice reading their papers several times aloud to partners while focusing on being fluent. After several "rehearsals," have students share their papers with the class. Praise students when they are expressive, clear, fluent, etc.

What I Like about School

fluency reproducible for
Ramona Quimby, Age 8

Name_____ Date_____

Fill in the blanks below. Then, practice reading the passage fluently. Remember to pause at punctuation, use an expressive voice, and speak in a clear, natural way.

In the book *Ramona Quimby, Age 8*, the main character had some good experiences in third grade, like when Mrs. Whaley told her that her jar label was neat and when she did a great book report. She also had some bad ones—really bad! The time she broke a raw egg all over her head was terrible! Then, there was the day she got really sick and threw up in the classroom. Yuck! Poor Ramona!

I have also had some good and bad experiences in third grade. One of the good things was when _____

_____

_____

_____

Another good thing that happened was _____

_____

_____

_____

_____

But, there was one bad thing that happened to me in third grade. What happened was

_____

_____

_____

_____

_____

_____

Comprehension Activities
for *Ramona Quimby, Age 8*

Pre-reading Activity: This activity gives students a purpose for reading, helps them monitor comprehension as they read, and teaches them to think critically about story elements and characters. Divide students into pairs and give each pair a copy of the What's Going to Happen? reproducible (page 117). Instruct each pair to come up with a list of questions they hope to find answers to as they read the book. Direct students to use the title, cover, table of contents, and blurb when formulating their questions. For example, why is it so important that she is eight years old? Does Ramona like Mrs. Whaley? Why did Ramona throw up? What is a "hard-boiled egg fad"? After pairs have created lists of questions, consider letting students share a few questions to see if pairs have any in common. Have pairs keep the questions list and record any answers they find in the reading.

During-reading Activity: Tell students that Beverly Cleary uses vivid descriptions and many details to help the reader "see," "hear," and "feel" everything that happens in the book. This helps the reader visualize, or "see" in her "Brain TV," what is happening. Visualizing is an important strategy that helps comprehension. Find examples of Cleary's vivid details throughout the reading, such as when Ramona's dad gives her an eraser in chapter 1 or when Ramona is sick in chapter 6. Point out to students how details such as these help them see, hear, and feel along with the character. Have students select an excerpt from the book which they find particularly descriptive. Encourage them to pick a section with details that they are able to "see" clearly and vividly in "Brain TVs." Have students close their eyes as you read the scene aloud, or have them read their own scenes as they visualize. Give each student a sheet of paper on which to draw what she visualized. Encourage students to include every detail possible. Then, have students copy the words, phrases, and sentences from the scene that helped them visualize easily.

Post-reading Activity: Give each student 10 index cards. Have students review the novel chapter by chapter to find the most important events. Then, have students make sequence-of-events booklets. Instruct each student to summarize each main event in one or two sentences and write the summary on an index card. Remind students to include only the most important events, not the details. It will be particularly helpful for students to use the chapters as outlines, so each student will have a cover card plus nine sequence cards. Possible sequence: Ramona begins third grade; Ramona helps the family by getting along with Willa Jean; Ramona cracks an egg on her head and overhears Mrs. Whaley call her a nuisance; the Quimbys have an argument; the girls have to make dinner the following night; Ramona throws up in class; Ramona's mom stays home to take care of her; Ramona presents her book report as a commercial and finds out Mrs. Whaley does not think of her as a nuisance; the Quimbys go out to dinner and are treated by a stranger for being such a nice family. Finally, have students add illustrations, make covers, and staple the "pages" together.

What's Going to Happen?
comprehension reproducible for
Ramona Quimby, Age 8

Names _____ Date _____

Look at the title, cover, blurb, and table of contents. What are some questions you have about the story? What are you wondering as you preview the book? What do you want to know? Think of a list of questions you and your partner hope to find answers to while reading the book. Write the questions in the first column. Keep this page in a safe place. Then, as you find answers to some of your questions, write the answers in the second column. If there is a question that you can't find an answer to, write a big question mark instead.

Questions	Answers Discovered While Reading

Sarah, Plain and Tall
by Patricia MacLachlan

(Harper & Row, 1985)

This Newbery Medal winner is about a prairie family and Sarah, who answers Papa's ad for a wife and mother. Sarah immediately captivates the children, Anna and Caleb. The family wants Sarah to stay because she brings hope and love into their lives. The complex characters and rich language support the modern theme of changing family relationships.

Related books: *Caleb's Story* by Patricia MacLachlan (HarperTrophy, 2002); *Skylark* (sequel to *Sarah, Plain and Tall*) by Patricia MacLachlan (HarperTrophy, 1997)

Phonemic Awareness Activities
for *Sarah, Plain and Tall*

Pre-reading Activity: Read the title to students. Have them pronounce the word *tall*. Ask, "Does the a in this word make the long /a/ sound like in *tale* or the short /a/ sound like in *cat*?" Have students pronounce the word *tall* replacing the a sound with the long /a/ sound and the short /a/ sound. Explain that the consonant l has a controlling effect on the letter a because when the letter l follows the letter a, it controls the a's sound and changes it to the short /o/ sound, like in *talk* (depending on the pronunciation in your region). Ask students if the a makes the long /a/, short /a/, or controlled short /o/ sound in *blame, hat, false, call, train, fall, small, swallow, analyze*, etc.

During-reading Activity: Use the characters' correspondence for this activity to help students focus on a small amount of text. Remind students that when two or three consonants are together and you can hear their sounds, it is called a *consonant blend*. Program a word card for each student with one of the following consonant blends: bl, br, cl, cr, dr, fl, fr, gl, gr, pl, pr, sc, sk, sl, sm, sn, sp, st, sw, tr, tw, scr, spl, spr, squ, str. Review by having students repeat each consonant's sound, then combining to make the blends' sounds. Then, discuss how the Wittings and Sarah wrote letters in order to get to know each other. Read the letters aloud. Have students identify initial consonant blends by holding up the corresponding cards. For example, in the first letter Sarah writes to Jacob, there are words containing fr, br, tr, str, and st.

Post-reading Activity: Give students a way to identify basic phonemic rules within the context of literature. Give each student a copy of the Found: Phonemes reproducible (page 119). Review each phoneme. Have students skim the novel to find words that contain these phonemes. Then, have students illustrate the objects. For example, in the box containing the long /e/ sound, each student can draw the sea. For the box containing the short /e/ sound, each student can draw a shell like the one Sarah gave to Caleb.

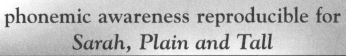

Found: Phonemes

phonemic awareness reproducible for

Sarah, Plain and Tall

Name_____ Date_____

In the novel, find words that contain the phonemes below. Draw one item in each box whose name represents the listed phoneme. Remember to select words that you can illustrate.

long /a/	long /e/	long /i/	long /o/
long /u/	short /a/	short /e/	short /i/
short /o/	short /u/	initial consonant blend	consonant digraph /sh/
consonant digraph /ch/	vowel team	hard c /k/	soft c /s/

Phonics Activities
for *Sarah, Plain and Tall*

Pre-reading Activity: Ask students to find the word in the title that contains the long /a/ sound (*plain*). Ask students what vowels represent the long /a/ sound in this word (ai). Tell students that these two letters make a vowel team and when two vowels are together, usually the "first one does the talking and the second keeps walking." Make letter cards with the letters a, i, p, l, and n. Have two students hold cards with the letters a and i, respectively. Since they will be the vowel team, have them link arms. Then, call up students to hold cards with the remaining letters. Demonstrate how students holding the p and l card should stand to the left of the vowel team and the student holding the n card should stand to the right of the vowel team to make the word *plain*. Point out how the a and i students do not move or break apart. Then, have a competition. Assign students to groups. Give each group the same letter cards: a, i, b, t, r, d, n, c, h, f, p, l. Have each group select two students to be the vowel team by holding the a and i cards. When you say go, have group members rearrange themselves to spell words with the ai vowel team. The first group to form a word receives one point. As groups create words, list them on the board so groups do not repeat words. If you have more students per group than letters, have those students serve as helpers to move people around, or let them record words on the board. Continue until students have created as many words as they can. The group with the most points wins. Possible words to build include *bait, braid, brain, chain, drain, faint, pain, nail, paint, pail, fail, tail, rail, trail,* and *hail*.

During-reading Activity: After reading a chapter, have a contest to find certain phonetic patterns in the text. Assign students to two teams. Select phonics rules that you have already gone over in class, and give verbal clues as to what students should find. For example, after reading chapter 2, have all students start at the beginning to find a word in which the letter y is used as a vowel (*pesky*). Instruct each student to skim the text and raise her hand when she finds a word. If the student responds correctly, give her team a point. This activity can be simplified for struggling readers by having students look for basic phonetic patterns such as long and short vowel sounds, hard/soft sounds of the letter g, words containing silent letters, etc. This activity can also be made more advanced with clues such as: find a word that contains a vowel digraph, find a word that has an r-controlled vowel, etc. Other ways to use this activity could be to have students skim only one page rather than a whole chapter, have students do this at the end of each chapter, or have students come up with the clues.

Post-reading Activity: This activity builds on the phonics pre-reading activity. Remind students that when two vowels work together as team, the first one usually "does the talking." Tell students that there are more vowel teams than just ai as in *plain*. Give each student a copy of the Vowel Teams reproducible (page 121). Have students read the sentences from the novels, decide what phonemes are missing, and circle the correct answers. Then, have students write the missing vowel teams in the blanks.

Vowel Teams

phonics reproducible for
Sarah, Plain and Tall

Name_____ Date_____

In the following sentences from the novel, some of the words contain vowel teams that have been left out. First, decide what sound would complete the incomplete words, and circle it. Then, fill in the blank with the correct vowel team.

1. "Caleb thought the story was over, and I didn't tell him what I had **r___lly** thought." (pages 4-5)

    r___lly: long /a/   long /e/   long /i/   long /o/   long /u/

2. "I looked at the long dirt **r___d** that crawled across the **pl___ns**, remembering the morning that Mama had died, **cr___l** and sunny." (page 5)

    r___d: long /a/   long /e/   long /i/   long /o/   long /u/
    pl___ns: long /a/   long /e/   long /i/   long /o/   long /u/
    cr___l: long /a/   long /e/   long /i/   long /o/   long /u/

3. "Yes, I can **br___d** hair and I can make stew and bake bread, though I prefer to build bookshelves and **p___nt**." (page 10)

    br___d: long /a/   long /e/   long /i/   long /o/   long /u/
    p___nt: long /a/   long /e/   long /i/   long /o/   long /u/

4. "'Did you bring some **s___**?' **cr___d** Caleb beside me." (page 19)

    s___: long /a/   long /e/   long /i/   long /o/   long /u/
    cr___d: long /a/   long /e/   long /i/   long /o/   long /u/

5. "A few **r___ndrops** came, gentle at first, then stronger and louder, so that Caleb and I covered our **___rs** and stared at **___ch** other without **sp___king**." (page 47)

    r___ndrops: long /a/   long /e/   long /i/   long /o/   long /u/
    ___rs: long /a/   long /e/   long /i/   long /o/   long /u/
    ___ch: long /a/   long /e/   long /i/   long /o/   long /u/
    sp___king: long /a/   long /e/   long /i/   long /o/   long /u/

Vocabulary Activities

for *Sarah, Plain and Tall*

re-reading Activity: The word and concept of *prairie* are important to students' understanding of *Sarah, Plain and Tall*. To help students envision this landscape during this time period, first have students share their guesses or existing background knowledge on prairies. Then, have a volunteer look up the word in a dictionary and read the definition to the class. Next, show photos of prairies from magazines, resource books, or the Internet. (If your classroom is in a prairie setting, have students go outside and imagine how the landscape would feel without any other buildings or roads in sight.) Tell students that Sarah comes from the coast, where she was used to living near the sea with forests of pine trees close by. Have students research and compare the two settings: the sea and coastal Maine, and the prairie. Have students illustrate each setting, labeling parts of the pictures that are different from each other.

uring-reading Activity: Have students look for story words that are not commonly used today that depict life during the era that is depicted in the book. For example, they may find the words *hearthstones, wagon, bonnet, paddock,* etc. Have students look up the words in dictionaries and share the definitions with the class. Then, allow a volunteer to draw a picture of each word. Display the pictures on a bulletin board titled "Pioneer Words."

ost-reading Activity: Ask students why they think Sarah described herself using the words *plain* and *tall.* Ask students to think of other words they might use to describe Sarah. List these words on the board. Remind students that describing words are called *adjectives.* Have students complete the Adjectives with Character reproducible (page 123) using adjectives to describe each character. Encourage each student to select two adjectives for each character that she thinks will best describe that character. For example, *independent* and *kind* are certainly more descriptive adjectives for Sarah than *plain* and *tall.* Then, have each student use the last box to list two adjectives that describe herself. Have students illustrate all of the characters and themselves. Display the illustrations on a bulletin board.

Adjectives with Character

vocabulary reproducible for

Sarah, Plain and Tall

Name_____ Date_____

Think of two adjectives that best describe each character. Write those in the blanks, following the same pattern as the book's title. Then, draw each character. In the last blanks, write your name and two adjectives that describe you. Draw a picture of yourself in the last box.

Sarah, _____ and _____

Papa, _____ and _____

Anna, _____ and _____

Caleb, _____ and _____

_____, _____ and _____

Fluency Activities
for *Sarah, Plain and Tall*

Pre-reading Activity: Discuss the fact that Anna and Caleb's father places an advertisement for a wife and mother. (Be sure to discuss the historical appropriateness of this!) Tell students that although they never get to read the actual ad he places, they can imagine what kinds of things Papa might have said. Then, have students practice their fluency by writing and reading ads for new family members. Model writing an ad before having students complete ads independently. Tell students that they will probably find it easier to read something aloud in a fluent manner when they have written it themselves. Have students use the Wanted: New Family Member reproducible (page 125) to write ads for new family members. Then, have students practice reading their ads aloud in pairs. Encourage students to focus on sounding natural, reading smoothly, not "chopping up" or stumbling over words, and pausing appropriately. After several practices, have students read their ads to the class.

During-reading Activity: While reading, take time to point out how the author uses "clues" to tell the reader how he should sound when reading aloud. For example, discuss the italics such as in "*I would have named you Troublesome.*" (*Sarah, Plain and Tall*, page 4). Discuss words the author uses when describing how the characters talk such as "'No,' said Papa slowly. 'Not a housekeeper'" (*Sarah, Plain and Tall*, page 8) and "'I am loud and pesky,' Caleb cried suddenly" (*Sarah, Plain and Tall*, page 54). When you encounter such "clues," discuss them with the class. Take time to reread these sections. Have students practice reading them as well, so they learn to focus on being appropriately expressive when reading dialogue.

Post-reading Activity: Have each student skim the novel to find her favorite part, then pair students. Have one partner in each pair be the listener and the other partner be the reader. When the reader reads her favorite part to the listener, have the listener write down one thing the reader did well and one thing she needs to practice. For example, the listener might say, "One thing you did right is that you read every word correctly. One thing you need to do is to slow down because you read very fast." Then, ask students to switch roles. After both students have had a turn, instruct the first reader to read her favorite part a second time while trying to follow the listener's advice. Switch roles again. Finally, reconvene as a class and discuss what students have learned about oral reading and whether they did better the second time after getting advice from the listeners.

First-Rate Reading™ Grade 3 • CD-0071 • © Carson-Dellosa

Name_____ Date_____

Write an advertisement for a new family member. Think about the qualities and characteristics you will want this new relative to have. Then, practice reading your ad aloud.

Jobs • Cars
Real Estate

Classifieds

Goods • Services
Lost and Found

Wanted

_____

_____

_____

_____

_____

_____

_____

_____

_____

_____

Pre-reading Activity: Explain the word *genre* to students. Write some common genres, such as *fiction*, *nonfiction*, *historical fiction*, *science fiction/fantasy*, *poetry*, etc., on the board. Have students name some of their favorite books and list the titles under the appropriate genres. Then, explain that any fictional book that is set in a past time period and has accurate historical elements is *historical fiction*. On a piece of chart paper, brainstorm a list of elements students can expect to find in a book to indicate that its genre is historical fiction. Possible examples would be a different style of language, illustrations that show period clothing, and descriptions of events that could have happened during a specific period of time. For this specific time period, students would find an absence of technologies that were not invented at the time, such as cars, telephones, computers, etc., as well as the presence of period technologies, such as wagons, manual farming and housekeeping, etc. Post the list for students to reference as they read.

During-reading Activity: Because many students will not have a great deal of existing knowledge about prairie life or the concept of advertising for a wife and mother, it is important to aid their comprehension. One way to do this is to have students actively read and think as they proceed through the novel. This will help them—and you—monitor their comprehension. Have students use the Active Reading reproducible (page 127) to actively read as they go through the novel. Students will keep track of developing problems, solutions, main events, and will also have an opportunity to respond to the reading. Make sure that students comprehend how the reproducible will help them to better understand what they read and how it may also demonstrate that they need to read some passages more than once.

Post-reading Activity: The characters in this story are at the heart of the book. This is an excellent book to discuss and learn about character development and the importance of characters' behaviors. Draw a web with the name *Sarah* in the middle. Have students skim through the book and list things that Sarah does and says which tell us about her personality. As students list examples, ask them what they think each behavior or comment says about Sarah. For example, discuss Sarah's response to Papa when he says the cat will "be good in the barn," and she says "She will be good in the house, too." (*Sarah, Plain and Tall*, page 19). What does this say about Sarah? Is she shy? Is she afraid to speak her mind? How does she feel about her cat? After students understand how to complete a web, have each student do a web for Sarah (using the class's responses plus new ones) and a web for one other character. Once the webs are complete, have students write short paragraphs about what they think the characters' behaviors and comments say about them.

Active Reading

comprehension reproducible for

Sarah, Plain and Tall

Name_____ Date_____

As you read the novel *Sarah, Plain and Tall*, stop after each reading session to fill in the chart below. If you are not able to fill in parts of the chart after reading, reread the text and see if that helps you understand it better and respond on the chart.

Pages or chapter read _____	Most important event from this reading
Problem/s happening right now	
	My thoughts on the reading
Possible solution/s for the problem/s	

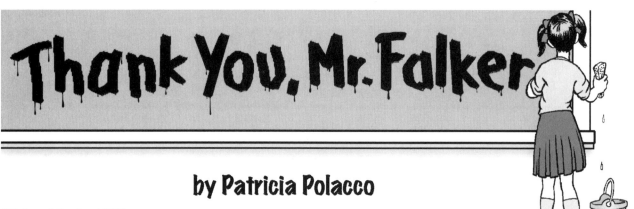

Thank You, Mr. Falker

by Patricia Polacco

(Philomel Books, 1998)

Little Trisha just can't make sense of words on a page. Other kids start to tease her and Trisha begins to hate school. In fifth grade, however, Mr. Falker discovers that Trisha has a learning disability and gets her a reading tutor. At the end, the author admits that she is Trisha. This book will inspire struggling students, and serve as a springboard to discuss reading, learning styles, and reading skills.

Related books: *Chicken Sunday* by Patricia Polacco (Paper Star, 1998); *The Keeping Quilt* by Patricia Polacco (Aladdin Library, 2001); *My Rotten Redheaded Older Brother* by Patricia Polacco (Aladdin Library, 1998)

Phonemic Awareness Activities
for *Thank You, Mr. Falker*

Pre-reading Activity: Read the excerpt where Trisha tries to sound out words ("the cah, cah. . . rrr, rrr. . .") (*Thank You, Mr Falker*, page 15). Ask, "What was Trisha trying to read?" ("The cat ran.") Say, "Th-th-a-a-n-n-k-k." Have students connect the phonemes to say "thank." Repeat with *bank*, *rank*, and *blank*. Ask what sound is heard repeatedly (ank). Have small groups brainstorm new words that end in ank. Then, ask students what the rime would be if the short /a/ was changed to a short /o/ or /u/ sound (ink, unk). Brainstorm words with these endings, as well.

During-reading Activity: Write *thank* on the board. Have students touch their throats and repeat the /th/ sound in *thank*. Ask if they feel vibrations in their throats. Write *they* on the board and have students say *they* with their fingers on their throats. Tell them the th consonant digraph can make the non-voiced /th/ sound as in *thank* or the voiced /th/ sound as in *they*. Explain that the vocal chords cause vibrations when forming the voiced /th/ sound. Brainstorm other words that begin with the th digraph and test them for the voiced /th/ sound or the voiceless /th/ sound. As students hear the /th/ phonemes while you read aloud, have them shake their hands to indicate vibration if they think a /th/ makes the voiced /th/. If /th/ is non-voiced, have them put their hands over their mouths. Use the Voiced and Non-Voiced Th reproducible (page 129) for extra practice.

Post-reading Activity: Write about 20 sentences from the book on sentence strips. Reread excerpts from the book. Have students volunteer to imitate how Trisha "broke" the words into sounds. Assign teams to play verbal charades. Have one student read a sentence strip, dividing the words into individual phonemes, so it is hard to understand. The remaining students must blend the phonemes together to decipher what the student is saying. The first team to join the phonemes correctly gets a point. When a student sounds out the phonemes incorrectly, discuss how that affects those who were guessing.

Voiced and Non-Voiced Th

phonemic awareness reproducible for
Thank You, Mr. Falker

Name_____ Date_____

Touch your throat with your fingers as you say each word aloud. If you feel a vibration, like in the word *they*, circle voiced. If you don't feel a vibration, like in the word *thank*, circle non-voiced.

think	voiced	non-voiced
throw	voiced	non-voiced
the	voiced	non-voiced
thin	voiced	non-voiced
them	voiced	non-voiced
though	voiced	non-voiced
theater	voiced	non-voiced
thick	voiced	non-voiced
those	voiced	non-voiced
thus	voiced	non-voiced
three	voiced	non-voiced
throw	voiced	non-voiced
than	voiced	non-voiced

Phonics Activities
for *Thank You, Mr. Falker*

Pre-reading Activity: Tell students that this story is about a girl named Trisha who has trouble reading and a teacher who helps her. Write the words *Trisha* and *teacher* on the board. (Consider writing on the board with a wet cloth, as Trisha did in the book.) Discuss what might cause a student to have trouble reading and the importance of knowing which letters make which sounds. Ask students what sound the letters s and h make in the name *Trisha*. Tell students that when the letters s and h are together, they make the /sh/ sound and it is called a consonant digraph. (If students did the phonemic awareness during-reading activity, remind them that th is a consonant digraph like sh.) Ask students what sound the letters c and h make in the word *teacher*. Have students say both digraphs, noting the differences in the sounds and the mouth/tongue/teeth placement. Have students work in pairs to think of and list as many words containing the ch and sh digraphs as they can. Let students share lists to see which pairs came up with the largest number of words.

During-reading Activity: This activity extends the pre-reading activity. Have students predict which digraph will show up more frequently in the text of *Thank You, Mr. Falker*. Have each student fold a sheet of paper in half vertically to make two columns, and label one column *sh* and the other *ch*. Then, have her circle the digraph she guesses will "win" (occur more in the text). As students read the story, have them tally the number of times they see the two digraphs. Encourage students to find the ch and sh digraphs in other words as they read various books and articles.

Post-reading Activity: Use Trisha's early writing and reading methods to review and assess class knowledge of phonics concepts. Discuss how Trisha learned to read with Miss Plessy and Mr. Falker. Have students practice their phonics skills like Trisha first demonstrated her reading and writing skills for Mr. Falker. Create a center with a small chalkboard, a sponge, a bowl of water, and a shoebox filled with sand. Tell students they will use the wet sponge to write different phonics elements on the chalkboard or their fingers to write in the sand. Take a turn with each student at the center or enlist a parent volunteer. Read the instructions on the Tactile Writing reproducible (page 131) to the student. As she completes each task, indicate on the reproducible whether she was successful. After each student has had a turn, talk about what method of writing students preferred and why. Compare the finger and sponge to a pencil, and the sand and chalkboard to paper.

Tactile Writing
phonics reproducible for
Thank You, Mr. Falker

Student's Name _____ Date _____

Read the directions (in **bold**) aloud to the student. Stop after each direction so that the student can complete the task. After the student finishes, note her performance as directed.

1. **Direction: Write the alphabet in uppercase letters.**
   Circle any letters the student writes incorrectly.
   A B C D E F G H I J K L M N O P Q R S T U V W X Y Z

2. **Direction: Write the alphabet in lowercase letters.**
   Circle any letters the student writes incorrectly.
   a b c d e f g h i j k l m n o p q r s t u v w x y z

3. **Direction: Write the letters that make the beginning sound in the word *thank*.**
   Did the student write *th*? _____ If not, what did the student write? _____

4. **Direction: Write the two consonants that make one sound (phoneme) in the word *Trisha*.**
   Did the student write *sh*? _____ If not, what did the student write? _____

5. **Direction: Write the letter that is silent in the word *dumb*.**
   Did the student write *b*? _____ If not, what did the student write? _____

6. **Direction: Write the letters that make the middle sound in *teacher*.**
   Did the student write *ch*? _____ If not, what did the student write? _____

7. **Direction: Write the letter that makes the beginning sound in *you*.**
   Did the student write *y*? _____ If not, what did the student write? _____

8. **Direction: Write the letters that make the middle sound in *mister*.**
   Did the student write *st*? _____ If not, what did the student write? _____

9. **Direction: Write the all of the vowels.**
   Did the student write *a, e, i, o, u*, and possibly *y* or *w*? _____
   If not, what did the student write? _____

Vocabulary Activities
for *Thank You, Mr. Falker*

Pre-reading Activity: Although there are plenty of illustrations in the book, there are also some challenging vocabulary words. Consider teaching the words *ladle, cooed, knowledge, miracle, dearest, torture, wobbly, two-tone, longed, elegant, slick, brilliant, stumbling, fault, maggoty,* and *cunning* before students read the book. Let students use the Our New Words reproducible (page 133) to record vocabulary word definitions. First, have each student choose an unknown word from the book, write it, and guess what it means. Then, have him look it up in a dictionary and write the definition. Finally, have him write a sentence using the word. Allow students to share definitions and discuss how the words might be used in the book.

During-reading Activity: While you are reading *Thank You, Mr. Falker,* pause on the first page and reread the family's saying: "Knowledge is like the bee that made that sweet honey. . ." (*Thank You, Mr. Falker,* page 2). Ask students what two things they are comparing in the sentence (*knowledge* and *bee*). Ask students how knowledge and the bee are the same. (They both have to be chased to get the reward.) Explain that when a sentence compares two nouns/things using the words *like* or *as,* it is called a *simile.* Tell students to listen for another simile in the book as you read ("She was reading like a baby. . .") (*Thank You, Mr. Falker,* page 15). After reading the book, have students use similes to describe the characters in the book ("Mr. Falker was as sweet as honey", "Trisha felt as a dumb as a dodo bird", "Eric was mean like an evil wizard", etc.). Then, have students write and illustrate similes that describe themselves. Compile them into a class book or display them on a bulletin board titled "Knowledge Is Like a Bee. . ."

Post-Reading Activity: After reading the story, discuss the family's tradition of tasting honey to represent sweet knowledge and its pursuit. Give each student a graham cracker with a spoonful of honey on top. (Be sure to get parents' permission first.) Have them dip their fingers into the honey and taste it. Tell them to pay particular attention to the taste and feel of the honey because they will be like Patricia Polacco and use vivid describing words. List responses students use to describe the honey (*sticky, sweet, gooey, thick, golden,* etc.). Tell students that these words are called *adjectives* and that writers use adjectives to help a reader visualize and feel what happens in a story. Reread several passages from the book and have students point out the adjectives. Tell students that you will name a noun and they must list as many adjectives to describe that noun as possible before you call "time." After each noun, have students share their adjectives. Some possible nouns to suggest are *sky, dog, woman, sand,* etc. Encourage students to use more adjectives in their writing.

Our New Words

vocabulary reproducible for
Thank You, Mr. Falker

Name_____ Date_____

On each line labeled Word, write a vocabulary word from the reading. On the lines labeled My guess, write what you think the words mean. On the lines labeled Dictionary definition, write meanings from a dictionary. On the last lines, write sentences using the words.

Word _____

My guess _____

Dictionary definition _____

Sentence _____

Word _____

My guess _____

Dictionary definition _____

Sentence _____

Word _____

My guess _____

Dictionary definition _____

Sentence _____

Word _____

My guess _____

Dictionary definition _____

Sentence _____

Word _____

My guess _____

Dictionary definition _____

Sentence _____

Fluency Activities

for *Thank You, Mr. Falker*

Pre-reading Activity: Discuss the difference between a fluent reader and a non-fluent reader. Ask students to list some characteristics of a non-fluent reader (choppy, gets "stuck" a lot, pauses too often, skips words, sounds out words slowly, etc.). Ask students to list characteristics of a fluent reader (sounds natural, is expressive, pauses at commas and periods, etc.). Tell students that they will be reading a story about a girl who is not a fluent reader. Ask students to discuss what they think a non-fluent reader might sound like while reading. Tell students to listen for how Trisha reads in the story and think about how Trisha's reading affected her comprehension.

During-reading Activity: As you read the story, pause whenever Trisha tries to read aloud in class or when it describes how she would stumble over words. Have students note how Trisha read. Reread those sections and discuss with students how reading in this manner affects comprehension, and how it made Trisha feel. Have students echo read as you demonstrate Trisha being non-fluent. Pause again when the book describes how "Sue Ellen. . . or Tommy Bob. . . read so easily" (*Thank You, Mr Falker*, page 11). Ask students how they think Sue Ellen and Tommy Bob sounded as they read. Have students volunteer to demonstrate Sue and Tommy reading. Finally, discuss how they think Trisha sounded after Mr. Falker helped her. Be sure to point out that the Trisha in the story is the young Patricia, who grew up to be the author of the book!

Post-reading Activity: Discuss how it took Trisha hard work and practice to learn how to read, even after Miss Plessy and Mr. Falker started helping her. Tell students that in order to be fluent, a reader must practice. Tell each student that he will have an opportunity to thank a teacher that helped him in school, and at the same time, students will get to practice fluency. Have each student write a letter on the Thank You reproducible (page 135) to thank a teacher or other grown-up who has taught him how to do something. (You may want each student to use a copy of the reproducible to write a draft, then revise and edit the writing, and finally copy the finished letter on a sheet of stationery.) After students have finished writing letters, have them practice reading them aloud. You may want to give students time to practice at home, as well. After students have had sufficient time to practice reading their letters fluently and with ease—like Sue Ellen and Tommy Bob in the story—have them present their letters to the class. Praise students when they read with appropriate pauses, intonations, and expression. To extend the activity, have students deliver or mail the letters to their intended recipients. Depending on your students' skill levels, you may need to add a short note to each letter to explain the assignment.

Thank You

fluency reproducible for
Thank You, Mr. Falker

Name_____ Date_____

Write a thank-you letter to a teacher or other adult who helped you learn to do something like Mr. Falker helped Trisha. Include details to explain how the person helped you. After you have finished writing, reread your letter aloud several times to practice your fluency. Remember to pause at the ends of sentences and wherever you added commas. Remember to use good expression and to read easily and naturally.

_____

_____

_____

_____

_____

_____

_____

_____

_____

_____

_____

Comprehension Activities
for *Thank You, Mr. Falker*

Pre-reading Activity: Tell students that in this book, the main character, Trisha, goes through a great deal of trouble because she can't read. She not only feels dumb and hates school, but her classmates tease her. Have each student think of a time when she was teased, made fun of, or laughed at. You may want to share a personal story at this point. Have each student write a journal entry about this experience. Have her include who teased her, why she was teased, how she felt, and what she did about it. Have volunteers share their journal entries before reading the story.

During-reading Activity: Tell students that sometimes an author won't describe a character just in words, but through the character's dialogue, behaviors, and thoughts. Pause as you read the story to have students fill in the Character Web reproducible (page 137) as a whole class. For example, for Trisha's behaviors students may suggest how she cried and hid under a stairwell, tricked the teachers, and liked to draw. For Trisha's dialogue, include statements like "Gramma, do you think I'm. . . different?" (*Thank You, Mr. Falker,* page 8) and "Thank you, Mr. Falker." For Trisha's thoughts, include how she "was afraid to turn any corner" (*Thank You, Mr. Falker,* page 21), she started believing that she was ugly and stupid, and how she hoped that the kids at her new school wouldn't know how dumb she was. Once the character web is complete, analyze it and discuss questions such as, "What does the author use most to tell us about the character—her behaviors, dialogue, or thoughts? What kind of person is Trisha? How would you describe her and why?"

Post-reading Activity: Explain that the book is autobiographical. Discuss how the author had trouble learning how to read but is now successful as a children's book writer. Have students share things they have had trouble learning but now are successful at (such as sports, school subjects, riding bikes, etc.). Have each student write an essay titled "When I Learned to. . ." Tell him to include details about what he was learning to do, why he had trouble, how he felt when he was struggling, how he finally managed to do it, and how he feels about it now. Then, have students illustrate their essays. Compile them into a class book or display on a bulletin board titled "Look at Us Now!"

Character Web

comprehension reproducible for
Thank You, Mr. Falker

Name_____ Date_____

Fill in the web bubbles with information about Trisha, the main character in *Thank You, Mr. Falker.*

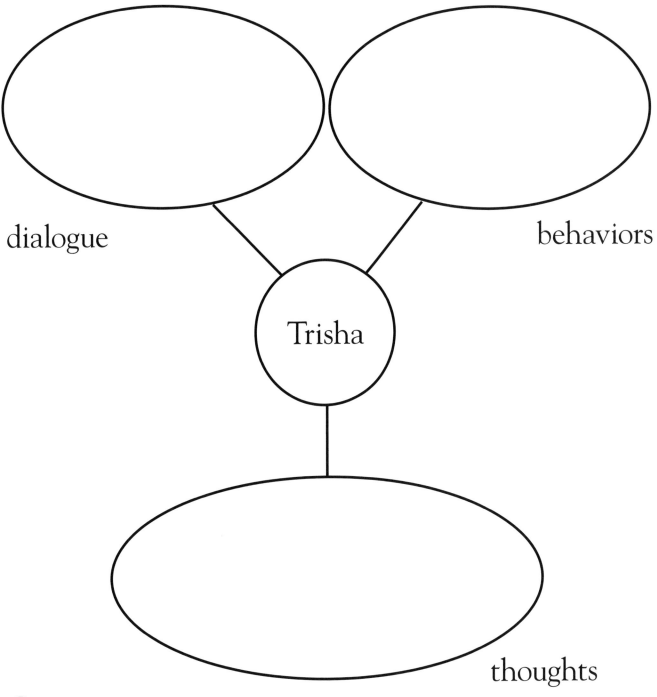

dialogue

behaviors

Trisha

thoughts

There's a Boy in the Girls' Bathroom
by Louis Sachar (Random House, 1994)

Bradley Chalkers is the worst kid in school, but Carla, the new school counselor, knows he can succeed if he tries. Carla's patience, faith, and kindness help Bradley transform from "a monster" to a self-confident, hard-working boy. Students relate to this book's themes and may recognize classmates who could use their kindness, too.

Related books: *Bad Times of Irma Baumlein* by Carol Brink (Macmillan, 1972) *Dear Mr. Henshaw* by Beverly Cleary (Bt Bound, 2000); *Harriet the Spy* by Louise Fitzhugh (Yearling, 2001); *Otherwise Known as Sheila the Great* by Judy Blume (Dell, 1993)

Phonemic Awareness Activities
for *There's a Boy in the Girls' Bathroom*

Pre-reading Activity: Have students name which words from the title have the /er/ phoneme (*there's* and *girls'*). Ask them to identify what graphemes make this sound (er and ir). Explain that these special vowel phonemes are called murmur or r-controlled vowels—the letter r is actually part of the phoneme. The r "controls" the vowel and changes its sound. Other r-controlled vowels include or as in *counselor*, ar as in *liar*, and ur as in *hurt*. On index cards, write these story words: *girl, there's, Chalkers, counselor, star, hurt, liar, Carla, stared, hard, distorted, squares, dollar, spitter, fourth, her, paper, barged, sister, cares, snickered, mother, fluttered, teacher, flabbergasted, tolerate, purple, father, asserted, smartest, hollered, behavior, form, perhaps, horror, warn, charming.* Ask a student to find a word card with an r-controlled vowel, such as the /er/ sound as in *girl.* Have him read the word, repeat the r-controlled vowel, and identify where it is and which graphemes represent it. Repeat until all cards are used.

During-reading Activity: While reading a chapter, select a phonemic skill to practice such as short /a/ phonemes in chapter 1, th consonant digraph in chapter 2, etc. Have groups find story words with the assigned phonemes. Select phonemic skills based on your students' abilities and needs, as well as your preferences and goals.

Post-reading Activity: On the board, copy the letter Bradley writes to Carla (*There's a Boy in the Girls' Bathroom,* pages 171-172). As you write, divide each word in the first sentence by its syllables and add appropriate syllable accent marks. Point out the syllables and accents. Explain that when students say words, some syllables have more "stress" or "accent" on them than others. For example, *Carla* has an accent on the first syllable. Say the word *Carla* correctly and have students repeat. Then, say *Carla* with stress on the second syllable and have them repeat. Repeat with each word in the first sentence to ensure students hear the difference between accented and unaccented syllables. Ask groups to copy additional sentences from the letter and add accent marks as necessary. Use the Syllables and Accents reproducible (page 139) for additional practice.

Syllables and Accents

phonemic awareness reproducible for
There's a Boy in the Girls' Bathroom

Name_____ Date_____

Divide the words listed below into syllables. Then, put accent marks over the stressed syllables. The first few words have been done for you. To help you figure out where the accent goes, say each word aloud, stressing different syllables each time, until the word sounds right.

Carla	Car'/la
color	co'/lor
wearing	wear'/ing
today	_____ / _____
sorry	_____ / _____
hundred	_____ / _____
percent	_____ / _____
arithmetic	_____ / _____ / _____ / _____
believe	_____ / _____
because	_____ / _____
hanging	_____ / _____
teaching	_____ / _____
kindergarten	_____ / _____ / _____ / _____
teacher	_____ / _____

Phonics Activities

for *There's a Boy in the Girls' Bathroom*

Pre-reading Activity: Assess students' abilities to sound-spell using vocabulary from *There's a Boy in the Girls' Bathroom*. Choose words from the book that are at least second-grade level and are complicated enough for students not to recognize them as sight words. Also, make sure that these words are not overly irregular in their spelling and that they comply with phonics rules you have taught students or feel they should know. Some possible words are *except, bulging, unrecognizable, counselor, sleeveless, ceramic, snickered, flabbergasted, modestly, corridor, geography, angrily, velvet, hesitated, impolite, belong, flunking, demanded, chicken, dispenser, cucumbers, concentrate, rather, sickening, passed, wonder, understood,* and *upset*. Have students sit at their desks with paper and pencils. Explain that you are giving them a diagnostic spelling test, not for grades, but to see what they understand about spelling. Call out words for them to spell, collect the papers, and prepare future phonics review lessons based on what students misspell from the list.

During-reading Activity: As students read, have them "collect" words from the book that fit the spelling and phonics rules you choose to review. Consider giving each student a different phonics rule for which to find words, based on the results of the spelling tests from the pre-reading activity. For example, if a student spelled *ceramic* with an s at the beginning, have him collect words that begin with the soft c sound such as *certainly, circle, cereal,* and *Cinderella*. When students have collected several words, check their lists. Then, have each student write his words on a piece of construction paper and write the rule at the top. Post the papers on a bulletin board for future reference.

Post-reading Activity: Assign students to teams. Review alphabetizing with first, second, and third letters. Give each team a copy of only the first section of the Alphabetical Order reproducible (page 141). Read the words and discuss how they relate to the story. Then, have groups race to see which group can correctly alphabetize the list the fastest. Mimic the point system in Mrs. Ebbel's class and at the birthday party by awarding two gold stars to the winning group and one star to the other two groups. Repeat for lists two and three. Finally, have groups race to alphabetize all three lists together. The team with the most words in the correct order wins. The correct order for each list is listed in the answer key (page 158).

First-Rate Reading™ Grade 3 • CD-0071 • © Carson-Dellosa

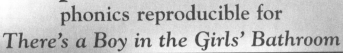

phonics reproducible for

There's a Boy in the Girls' Bathroom

Name_____ Date_____

Use this with the phonics post-reading activity.

List 1: Fishkin, Claudia, Andy, Chalkers, Lori, Colleen, Davis, Bartholomew, Melinda, Jeff, Mrs. Ebbel, Carla, Ronnie, Bradley

- -

List 2: library, bathroom, list, toilet, boy, counselor, girls', homework, liar, monster, teacher, basketball, office, school

- -

List 3: candles, heart, party, star, punch, book, presents, ribbon, letter, singing, frown, smile, birthday, love

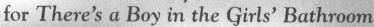

Vocabulary Activities
for *There's a Boy in the Girls' Bathroom*

Pre-reading Activity: Three of the most important vocabulary words (*lie, friend, counselor*) should be discussed prior to reading. Although these words are relatively simple, it is important that students discuss their meanings (especially for *friend* and *lie*) in order to set up the story. Have each student create a word web for each word, and take a few minutes to brainstorm and write any words or phrases that come to mind. Then, have students share by adding to a class web. Ask the following questions to guide the discussion on the first two vocabulary words: "What is a lie? What does it mean to be a liar? If you lie only once, are you a liar? Do grown-ups lie? What is 'a little white lie?' Is there a difference between a little lie and a big lie? What if a person only lies to impress someone or to make someone like them? What is a friend? What does it mean to be a friend? Can you buy friendship? What kinds of things do good friends do for each other? What kinds of behaviors would make you not want to be someone's friend? Is a person your friend if he lies to you? What if he apologizes?" For the last vocabulary word, *counselor*, have a student look up the word in a dictionary. Write the definition for *counsel* and *counselor* or discuss what a school counselor's job might be, and what students think a counselor should and should not do.

During-reading Activity: While reading, have students record new or interesting words and define them using context clues on copies of the Vocabulary Sharing reproducible (page 143). Then, have students meet in groups to share their vocabulary words and discuss the meanings they came up with. Consider modeling this process so that students understand not only the thinking process required to define the words, but also the conversations that should occur in their groups. For example, say, "In chapter 3 on page 15, I found the word *flabbergasted*. I picked that word because I liked how it sounded, and I had never heard it before. I think it means (reading off your paper) shocked or really surprised. The context clues I used are (again, referring to your paper) that his mom says she doesn't even know what time they feed the lions, and she even stumbles on her words, saying 'I-I don't even know. . .' to Bradley. So, it's like she can't believe Bradley said this. What do you guys think the word means?" Then, let other group members discuss and share their words. Once students know how to do this, it can be incorporated throughout this novel, as well as others.

Post-reading Activity: Review nouns, verbs, and adjectives. Discuss the characters of Bradley, Carla, and Jeff. Have each student write a biographical poem on one of the three characters using the following pattern:
  Line 1: one noun (for example, *counselor*)
  Line 2: three verbs (for example, *cares, shares, listens*)
  Line 3: five adjectives (for example, *friendly, confident, honest, calm, gentle*)
  Line 4: one noun (for example, *friend*)
Challenge students to use very specific words. Encourage the use of thesauruses and dictionaries. Have each student title her poem with the character's name and add an illustration of the character. Display them on a bulletin board titled "Complex Characters."

Vocabulary Sharing
vocabulary reproducible for
There's a Boy in the Girls' Bathroom

Name_____ Date_____

While reading, select words that are unfamiliar, new, or interesting. Then, use context clues to define them. Be ready to share your words, definitions, and how you came up with them with your group later.

Chapter ____ Page ____ Word _____

Sentence from the book: _____

_____

Your definition: _____

_____

Context clues: _____

_____

Chapter ____ Page ____ Word _____

Sentence from the book: _____

_____

Your definition: _____

_____

Context clues: _____

_____

Chapter ____ Page ____ Word _____

Sentence from the book: _____

_____

Your definition: _____

_____

Context clues: _____

_____

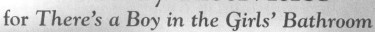re-reading Activity: Tell students that this novel contains scenes with a variety of emotions such as anger, embarrassment, fear, excitement, etc. The main character tries to be very tough and mean. He often pretends he doesn't care about anything. Discuss how a person might sound reading the dialogue for such a character, as well as how a person might read a scene in which the characters are embarrassed, teasing each other, fighting, etc. Tell students to listen for these emotions in the main character's "voice" when you read aloud and to keep this in mind when they read aloud or silently.

uring-reading Activity: Direct students to select an emotionally charged scene such as when Bradley argues with his parents in chapter 3, when Jeff goes into the girls' bathroom in chapter 6, or the fight after school in chapter 14. Reread the scene, directing students to note your expression, voice intonations, etc. When you are finished, ask students to name some of the things they noticed that you did while reading aloud that made you fluent. Then, have students split into pairs and take turns rereading the scene. Encourage students to try all of the things they mentioned about your oral reading. Circulate around the room and listen for particularly fluent readers.

ost-reading Activity: Go back to the letters Carla and Bradley wrote to each other. Have students reread them aloud. Then, have students use the Letter from a Friend reproducible (page 145) to write Carla's response to Bradley. Give students time to practice reading their letters aloud. After they feel that they are reading the letters fluently, let each student record himself reading it. Have students play back their readings and listen while following along in their letters. Direct students to note any errors, inappropriate pauses, etc. Have each student write one thing he did well in his oral reading and one thing he needs to improve. Suggest that students think about expression, smoothness, stumbling, pausing, etc., as they review how they did.

Letter from a Friend
fluency reproducible for
There's a Boy in the Girls' Bathroom

Name_____ Date_____

In the space below, write Carla's next letter to Bradley. Refer to his letter, and try to answer his questions or comment on his news.

Dear Bradley,

_____

_____

_____

_____

_____

_____

_____

_____

_____

Love, Carla

Practice reading your letter aloud a few times. Remember to keep these tips in mind:
* Don't read too fast or too slowly. Use the same speed you would use while talking.
* Pause at commas and ending punctuation.
* Use good expression.
* Make sure your voice is loud and clear.
* Be comfortable enough with your words so that you don't stumble or get stuck.
* Try to sound as natural as possible.

Next, record yourself reading the letter. Play it back. Did you make any mistakes? Did you "eat" any periods or commas? Did you use the tips above? On the lines below, write one thing you noticed about your oral reading that was great and one thing you need to improve.

One thing I do well when I read aloud is _____

_____

One thing I could do better when I read aloud is _____

_____

Comprehension Activities
for *There's a Boy in the Girls' Bathroom*

Pre-reading Activity: The title of this novel always catches students' attention. After sharing the title, cover, and back cover blurb, have students write predictions about who goes into the girls' bathroom and why. Let each student share his prediction. Tell students to keep these predictions handy because they might be surprised when they read the novel! Then, revisit and discuss the predictions after reading chapter 6.

During-reading Activity: It is critical to have discussions throughout this novel to ensure that students understand some of the critical events, as well as get the opportunity to think about and discuss some of the characters' behaviors and possible motives. Use the questions below as discussion starters.

Chapters 1 - 10
- What do you think of Mrs. Ebbel so far?
- Why do you think Bradley talks to his "animal friends?"
- What is your opinion of Carla?
- What kind of relationship do Bradley's parents seem to have?
- Discuss Carla and Bradley's first meeting.

Chapters 11 - 20
- In chapter 11, why do you think Jeff stopped himself from saying "I can help you with your homework," to Bradley?
- Why do suppose Bradley doesn't want anyone else to like Jeff?
- Why do you think Bradley told his mother that Jeff beat him up?
- Why do you think Jeff thought he couldn't be friends with Bradley **and** the other boys?
- Carla says a lot of people don't think counselors belong in schools. What do you think?

Chapters 21 - 35
- What do you think of Bradley's list of topics to discuss with Carla? What would your list have?
- Bradley wakes up determined to "be good" in chapter 25. What happens? How did you feel while reading it?
- What are some details that prove Bradley is starting to change?

Chapters 36 - 47
- During the meeting with the parents and Carla, a school board member says "You don't have to keep promises to children." What do you think of that statement?
- Why do you think Bradley gets angry with Carla when she tells him she is leaving?
- How did you feel about the ending of the book?

Post-reading Activity: Tell students that they will be creating character portraits that represent the characters' personalities, feelings, problems, etc. Distribute copies of the Character Portraits reproducible (page 147). Have each student represent a character in each square. Tell students that when they are finished with their portraits, a person who has never read the book should be able to look at them and "know" what the characters are like. Students may use words, pictures, phrases, etc. to depict their characters. Encourage students to go back through the book for ideas.

Character Portraits
comprehension reproducible for
There's a Boy in the Girls' Bathroom

Name_____ Date_____

Make character portraits that represent each character's personality, feelings, problems, etc. When you are finished with the portraits, a person who has never read the book should be able to look at them and "know" what the characters are like. You may add words, pictures, phrases, etc. from the book to depict the characters.

Bradley	Carla
Jeff	a character of your choice

Why Mosquitoes Buzz in People's Ears
by Verna Aardema

(The Dial Press, 1975)

This cumulative folktale describes a chain of events set off by a mosquito's nonsense lie and ending with a mother owl's baby getting killed. The King Lion holds a meeting in order to find out what has happened, and the mosquito flees to avoid punishment. Ever since, the mosquito has had a guilty conscience and has buzzed in people's ears to find out if everyone is still angry with him.

Related books: *Bringing the Rain to Kapiti Plain* by Verna Aardema (Puffin, 1992); *Who's in Rabbit's House? A Masai Tale* by Verna Aardema (Dial, 1992); *Why the Sun and the Moon Live in the Sky* by Elphinstone Dayrell (Houghton Mifflin, 1990)

Phonemic Awareness Activities
for *Why Mosquitoes Buzz in People's Ears*

Pre-reading Activity: In the book *Why Mosquitoes Buzz in People's Ears*, the animals make noises as they move. To help readers "hear" these noises, the author has used *onomatopoeia*—words that sound like what they mean. Before reading the story, flip through the pages, show students the animals, and ask, "What noise would an iguana make when it moves?" After students offer possibilities, say, "The iguana in this book makes this noise when it moves: *mek, mek*. Say *mek*." Then, ask students what phonemes they hear in this word (/m/, /e/, /k/). Repeat for all of the animal sounds.

During-reading Activity: Although identifying initial consonants is a fairly basic activity, many struggling readers are still developing this simple skill. Review initial sounds using the story animals. Make enough copies of the Animals Animals reproducible (page 149) for each student to get a card. Cut out the cards and distribute them randomly. Tell each student to hold up her card when she hears a story word that begins with the same sound as the one on her card.

Post-reading Activity: Ask students how the problem in the story began. (The iguana didn't want to listen to the mosquito's nonsense.) Discuss how not listening can cause problems. The lion helped solve the problem by listening. Tell students that they will be like the lion for this activity. Give one picture card from the Animals Animals reproducible (page 149) to each student. Select one student to be the "listening lion." Have students stand in a circle. Blindfold the "listening lion" and have him stand in the middle. Whisper an initial phoneme in his ear. Then, have each student make the initial sound of the picture name on her cards. The "lion" should listen for the same sound, and when he hears it, point at that person. That person is the next "lion." Have students swap cards before the next "lion" takes a turn.

Animals Animals

phonemic awareness reproducible for
Why Mosquitoes Buzz in People's Ears

Name_____ Date_____

Use these cards with the phonemic awareness during-reading and post-reading activities (page 148).

Phonics Activities
for *Why Mosquitoes Buzz in People's Ears*

Pre-reading Activity: Read the title to students. Ask them to share their thoughts on mosquitoes. Write the word *mosquito* on the board. Point out to students that the /k/ sound in *mosquito* is represented by the letters qu. Tell students that the letter q is almost always followed by the letter u. Challenge students to find the phonetic pattern for qu. (Qu makes the blended sound /kw/ as in *quake*, or /k/ as in *mosquito*.) Provide each student with a copy of the Team Q and U reproducible (page 151) which lists the words *question, opaque, quake, unique, quiz, square, bouquet, conquer, squeak, quilt, clique,* and *squid*. Have students sort the words according to the sounds the qu makes.

During-reading Activity: Tell students that this book is about many beasts or creatures, and that the trouble starts when an iguana puts sticks in his ears so he can't hear the mosquito complaining. Write the words *beasts, creatures, ears,* and *hear* on the board and repeat them. Then, ask students to find the phonetic pattern in the words. (They all have the long /e/ sound spelled with ea.) Point out how the long /e/ is represented with the vowels ea, and tell them that when two vowels are together, they are a *team*. (Usually the first one "does the talking, while the second one keeps walking.") Give a word card with the letter e to one student and a word card with the letter a to another. Have the students link arms and walk together. Then, have them pause while the first student "talks" his letter name and the other one keeps "walking." Tell students that other vowel teams follow this pattern, too. Demonstrate with word cards for the following vowel teams: ai, ay, ea, ee, oa, and ue. On the board, list at least one word with each vowel pattern. Then, have students look for and list vowel team words while reading the story. When a student finds a vowel pattern word, have her pause and say the word, stressing the long vowel sound.

Post-reading Activity: This activity gives students the opportunity to extend the above activity in a kinesthetic manner and work as teams like vowels do. Divide students into six groups. Give each group a card with one of the following teams: ai, ay, ea, ee, oa, ue. Also, give each group cards with various consonants. Have two students per group serve as the vowel team by holding the vowel team card and linking arms. Have the rest of the group members each hold one consonant card. Tell students that when you say "Go!" the group members must sort themselves in a way to spell words using the vowel teams and some of the additional consonants. When you call "Time!" each group who has formed a word correctly will receive a point. You may want to do one practice run before awarding points.

Team Q and U

phonics reproducible for
Why Mosquitoes Buzz in People's Ears

Name_____ Date_____

No question, q and u go together! Sort these qu words according to the sounds the two letters make. Write the words in the correct columns. Then, think of some words of your own or use a dictionary to find more words that contain the letters qu. Write those words in the correct columns as well.

Word bank: opaque, quake, unique, quiz, square, bouquet, conquer, squeak, quilt, clique, squid

/kw/ like in *question*	/k/ like in *mosquito*
_____	_____
_____	_____
_____	_____
_____	_____
_____	_____
_____	_____
_____	_____
_____	_____
_____	_____
_____	_____

Vocabulary Activities
for *Why Mosquitoes Buzz in People's Ears*

Pre-reading Activity: Before reading *Why Mosquitoes Buzz in People's Ears*, it is important that students understand the concept of a folktale. Tell students that they will be reading a story that is a folktale. Brainstorm things that students already know or think they know about folktales. Confirm or correct their ideas, and give examples of other folktales. Tell students to look for some folktale characteristics as you read the story, such as their cumulative and repetitive nature, their explanation of things in nature, influence from other countries or cultures, and the presence of fantasy or "tall" elements.

During-reading Activity: As you read the story, pause when the lion meets with the animals, and reread the lion's words, "So, it was the mosquito who annoyed. . ." (*Why Mosquitoes Buzz in People's Ears*, page 21). Ask students to identify all of the verbs in the lion's dialogue (*annoyed, frightened, scared, startled, alarmed, killed, wake*). Review, if necessary, what a verb is. Talk about the meaning of each word. Ask students if any of the verbs mean almost the same thing (*frightened/scared/startled/alarmed*). Tell students that these words are *synonyms*. Ask them to think of other synonyms for *frightened/scared/ startled/alarmed* (*terrified, spooked, panicked*). As a class, come up with other words the lion could have used in his dialogue. Reread the dialogue using the new synonyms. For example, "So, it was the mosquito who bothered the iguana, who spooked the python, who. . ."

Post-reading Activity: Have each student select one animal from the story and contribute to a class book of verbs that describes actions the animal may do. For example, the mosquito may have *buzzed, flown, bit, zipped, annoyed, bugged*, etc. Use the Book of Verbs reproducible (page 153) to help students complete this activity. Have each student choose an animal from the story, write the name of the chosen animal on the line, then add a verb to complete the sentence. Repeat the process in the rest of the numbered boxes and illustrate the animal doing each of the actions. Then, have students cut the boxes and staple them together to create books of verbs. Encourage the use of thesauruses and review correct past tense verb spellings. Bind all of the books together to create a class book of verbs.

Book of Verbs

vocabulary reproducible for
Why Mosquitoes Buzz in People's Ears

Name_____ Date_____

On the first line in each box below, write the name of an animal from the book. Then, on each second line, write a verb that the animal could do. Illustrate the animal performing the action in each box. Then, cut out the boxes and attach them with a staple or paper clip. Flip the pages of your book to see what your animals are doing.

The _____ _____ .
(animal)   (verb)

The _____ _____ .
(animal)   (verb)

The _____ _____ .
(animal)   (verb)

The _____ _____ .
(animal)   (verb)

Fluency Activities
for *Why Mosquitoes Buzz in People's Ears*

Pre-reading Activity: Tell students that you will read a sentence to them and they will have to determine your feelings based on the way you read the sentence. Read the sentence "I did it!" in an excited, happy tone. Ask students to guess how you feel, how they knew, and what the scenario could be. (In other words, what did you do that you are happy and excited about?) Then, read the sentence again, this time with a defeated, sighing tone. Again, ask students to guess your feelings, how they knew, and what the situation might be. Repeat the sentence in various ways: angry and defensive, guilty and embarrassed, etc. Help students note how although the words were exactly the same, your expression, tone, volume, etc., determined how you felt and gave clues about the situation. Tell students that this is why it is so important for them to read with expression and in a realistic way—to accurately express characters' feelings. Explain that authors use clue words to help readers figure out how characters should sound. For example, if an author says ". . . the character begged," that character's dialogue should be read in a pleading way. The characters in *Why Mosquitoes Buzz in People's Ears* have some misunderstandings and disagreements, so there are times in the story when certain characters are upset or defensive. Tell students to listen carefully (if you plan to read the book aloud) and notice your expressions and the words the author uses to give the reader clues about characters' feelings.

During-reading Activity: This story lends itself to choral reading because of its rhythmic repetition. Tell students to read the repetitive lines in the story ("So, it was. . .") chorally with you. Point out how there should be a rhythm to the lines and demonstrate how the punctuation helps you establish that rhythm. Provide feedback and praise to students, and allow those who you hear reading fluently and rhythmically to demonstrate.

Post-reading Activity: Tell students that many folktales have repetitive text because they make the story interesting to tell orally. Remind students that folktales, legends, fairy tales, etc., have been around for so long because the stories have been passed down orally, like traditions, from generation to generation. Discuss what makes a good storyteller. Review the book's illustrations and find the red bird that is "just listening" to the story on each page. Tell students that part of being a good storyteller is being a fluent reader because it inspires others to listen. Ask students if they would enjoy hearing you read a story in a monotone, choppy voice. (Demonstrate, if desired.) Give half of the students copies of Passage 1 from the Telling a Story reproducible (page 155). Give the remaining students copies of Passage 2. Tell students that they will practice reading their passages aloud until they are confident that they can share their stories in fluent, interesting ways that will capture and maintain the listeners' interest. After students have had sufficient time to practice their passages, let each student read to a student who had a different passage.

Telling a Story

fluency reproducible for
Why Mosquitoes Buzz in People's Ears

Name_____ Date_____

Practice reading the passage below. When you feel you can read the passage fluently and with ease, present the story to a partner. Remember to be expressive and try to show the characters' feelings.

Passage 1: I Want a Puppy

Once there was a boy named Steven who wanted a puppy more than anything else in the whole world. Everyday he'd beg his mom, "Please, Mom. I promise I'll take care of him. I promise I'll feed him and walk him and bathe him. I'll do everything! You won't even know he's here!"

"Oh, honey, I don't know," his mom sighed one night. "A dog is a lot of work."

"I know, Mom, I know!" Steven tried to convince his mother. "I'll make a deal with you. Let me prove to you that I can do it. I'll be responsible, I promise! If after a month, I'm not taking care of the dog, you can take him back to the pet shop."

"Well. . ." Mom hesitated.

Steven jumped on the chance. "Please, pretty please!" He threw his arms around her neck, and Mom laughed.

"Oh, all right," she gave in. "But, if you break your promise. . ." she warned.

"Oh, I won't! I won't!"

Practice reading the passage below. When you feel you can read the passage fluently and with ease, present the story to a partner. Remember to be expressive and try to show the characters' feelings.

- -

Passage 2: The Annoying Mosquito

Once there was a mosquito who decided he wanted to annoy the other animals in the forest. He went around, from animal to animal, buzzing in their ears. The first animal was a small rabbit. "Stop buzzing in my ear!" the rabbit squeaked. The second animal was a sleepy chimp. "Stop buzzing in my ear!" the monkey howled.

The next animal was a boa constrictor. "Stop buzzing in my ear!" hissed the snake. By this time, the mosquito was having quite a bit of fun. The next animal he went to was the mighty lion. "Stop buzzing in my ear!" roared the lion, and he squished the mosquito with one swift stomp of his paw. And, that was the last animal the mosquito annoyed!

Pre-reading Activity: Tell students that many times a story can get distorted and confused, which causes misunderstandings. Tell students that they will be playing "Telephone." You will whisper something to one student, and that student will repeat it to the next student, and so on, until the last person says aloud what he was told. Usually, the final statement(s) will be very different from the original. Tell students that the story they are going to read is similar to "Telephone" in that the version of the event told at the end of the story is very different from the original event. Read the first page to students and have them predict how they think the story will end. Write down a few predictions and revisit them after reading the book.

During-reading Activity: Give each student several 8" x 1" strips of construction paper and glue or tape. Explain that in this book, each event causes another event to happen, making a chain of events. Have students demonstrate a chain by linking arms. Tell students that as you read the story, they are to look for the events that make other events happen. Have each student write each event in his own words on a strip of paper and glue it into a link. Then, have him connect each subsequent event to the previous one to create a chain of events from the story. This shows how the events connect and build upon each other. As you read, stop to discuss the events and give time for students to make their links.

Post-reading Activity: Discuss the characteristics of a folktale and whether students think this is a true story explaining why mosquitoes buzz in people's ears. Have students think of natural occurrences such as thunder, earthquakes, etc. List these web-style on the board so that there are several ideas from which students can select. Direct each student or pair of students to select one natural occurrence and write a folktale explaining it. Guide students to write them in cumulative form with repetitive lines. Remind students that many folktales have messages or lessons. Ask students to think about what the message or lesson might be in this book. (The chain of events started with mosquito's lie, so the moral of the story is *Don't lie*.) Use copies of the Lessons Learned reproducible (page 157) for students to record the lessons that could be learned from their stories. Display on a bulletin board titled "Lesson Learned."

Lessons Learned

comprehension reproducible for
Why Mosquitoes Buzz in People's Ears

Name_____ Date_____

Fill in the writing prompts below about the folktale you wrote.

My story explains the event _____

I think the lesson in my story is _____

_____

because _____

_____

The way I can apply the lesson to real life is _____

_____

Illustrate a scene from your story below.

Answer Key for Activity Pages

This answer key includes information for pages that have definite answers, as well as the names of the pictures students will use. Answers are not included for games, drawing activities, activities in which students hold up cards during-reading, storytelling activities, manipulative spelling activities, and other activities in which individual and group participation are oral. Also, at this level (grade 3), answers for activities where students must find information from the novel, such as discussion question answers, spelling patterns, etc., do not have answers because the answers will vary widely.

Because of Winn–Dixie by Kate DiCamillo

page 21: Everyone, like, invite, like, one, goes, Gone, there, barbecue, there, great, There, Pie, theme, great, orange, juice, grapefruit, juice, have, Hope, come, and Sincerely should be highlighted. Note that answers will vary depending on your phonics program's definition of silent e. It may be more effective for you to make an individual answer key for this page.

page 23: Students can make the following words: kindness, kinder, careful, careless, endless, painful, painless, hopeful, hopeless, thankful, thankless, colorful, colorless, darker, darkness, singer, painter, sadness.

page 25: Several sentences have more than one answer. The most common answers are listed below. Accept reasonable responses but note how the meanings are different according to the punctuation. 1. I told the preacher to write down what we needed at the store, and that was bread, butter, eggs, tuna, fish sticks, milk, bones for the dog, and honey. 2. On the right, wall tapestries are hung. 3. He said, "Mary, Anne, are you all right?" 4. It was a sunny, windy day, and leaves blew off the trees into the street. 5. Things I won't eat include coconut cake, chocolate pie, and celery. 6. She saw the boy who entered the room, and shuddered. 7. My brother Tom likes pancakes for dinner. 8. Lynnette, my sister needs to mow the lawn.

The Chalk Box Kid by Clyde Robert Bulla

page 29: Change, say, and take should be highlighted in yellow. Hat, at, and apple should be highlighted with orange. Walk, crawl, false, talk, watch, call, want, bawl, and ball should be highlighted with pink.

page 37: Chapter titles are: The Room, Uncle Max, The New School, The Burned Building, A Party, Mr. Hiller, Gregory's Garden, "Nothing at All," Ivy and Richard

Charlotte's Web by E. B. White

page 39: /sh/ = Michigan, Charlotte, Chicago, machine; /ch/ = chore, couch, reach, orchard, chariot, each, teach, chair, chocolate, chilly, children, peach, channel, ouch; /k/ = chemical, character, stomach, echo, schedule, technical, chorus, orchestra, ache, chemistry

Freckle Juice by Judy Blume

page 49: Answers will vary depending on your regional dialect. Oo words include cruise, true, fruit, suit, glue, due, chew, attitude, tune, and flute. Long u words include few, fume, argue, human, and value.

Judy Moody by Megan McDonald

page 69: Down answers: 1. rare 3. Todd 5. Stink 7. flag 9. tp Across answers: 2. Jaws 4. Mouse 6. bad 7. Frank 8. gnat

page 73: Antonyms are: open-closed (or shut); laughing-crying; huge-tiny (or small); smooth-rough (or bumpy); under-over; dark-light

Answer Key for Activity Pages

The Legend of the Indian Paintbrush by Tomie dePaola

page 78: The words for the pre-reading activity index cards are plains, father, age, decorate, path, same, as, warriors, place, maiden, paints, great, shall, day, made, sank, dark, hairs, tails, gathered, frames, remained, satisfied, share, gave, awoke, created, awake, faithful, shall, watch, gazed, happy, ablaze, sang, and praises.

page 81: In order, the answers are wren, wrist, write, wrong, wrench, wrapper, wreck, wreath, and wrinkle. Students should write the letters wr in each blank.

page 83: Possible compound words are playground, underground, sunset, downhill, downside, downstairs, homework, playroom, goodbye, classroom, homeroom, paintbrush, buckskin, and underbrush.

Lon Po Po: A Red-Riding Hood Story from China by Ed Young

page 89: Students should use manipulatives to indicate number of phonemes. once = 4, woman = 5, who = 2, three = 3, children = 7, old = 3, wolf = 4, dusk = 4, grandmother = 9, po = 2, light = 3, sweet = 4, hemp = 4, basket = 6, hairy = 3, visit = 5, lon = 3, gingko = 4

Mr. Popper's Penguins by Richard and Florence Atwater

page 101: Connected penguins should make these words: sitting, strutting or strutted, ringing, dragging, running, tripping or tripped, regretted or regretting, flapping or flapped, squatting or squatted, occurred, stopped or stopping, putting. (Any combination of these is correct as long as the words are correct and all of the penguins are used.)

Ramona Quimby, Age 8 by Beverly Cleary

page 109: Students should sort cards into these categories: gh makes the /f/ sound = tough, laughed, cough, enough; gh makes the hard /g/ sound = spaghetti, ghastly; gh is silent = right, high, daughters, sighed, through, sight, thought, ought, eight.

page 111: 1. If students do not use the to alphabetize, the titles in alphabetical order are: At Howie's House, The Extra-good Sunday, The First Day of School, The Hard-boiled Egg, The Patient, The Quimbys' Quarrel, Rainy Sunday, Ramona's Book Report, Supernuisance 2. The words in alphabetical order are: Beezus, commercial, egg, Howie, Mrs. Kemp, nuisance, Ramona, Sunday, throw up, tongue, Yard Ape

page 113: Answers will vary; some may not be found exactly in the dictionary because the usage is idiomatic. Basic definitions are: 1. Drop = stop 2. paid = gave 3. saw = talked to, ran into, visited 4. kind = type 5. fly = go through the air 6. mean = intend 7. stamped = struck against the ground 8. hand = give to someone

Sarah, Plain and Tall by Patricia MacLachlan

page 121: 1. really = long /e/ 2. road = long /o/, plains = long /a/, cruel = long /u/ 3. braid = long /a/, paint = long /a/ 4. sea = long /e/, cried = long /i/ 5. raindrops = long /a/, ears = long /e/, each = long /e/, speaking = long /e/

Thank You, Mr. Falker by Patricia Polacco

page 129: voiced = the, them, though, those, thus, than; non-voiced = think, throw, thin, theater, thick, three, throw

There's a Boy in the Girls' Bathroom by Louis Sachar
page 139: Students should write words to indicate the following syllabication = to/day', sor'/ry, hun'/dred, per/cent', a/rith'/me/tic, be/lieve', be/cause', hang'/ing, teach'/ing, kin'/der/gar/ten, teach'/er
page 141: Students should alphabetize lists as follows: List 1 = Andy, Bartholomew, Bradley, Carla, Chalkers, Claudia, Colleen, Davis, Fishkin, Jeff, Lori, Melinda, Mrs. Ebbel, Ronnie; List 2 = basketball, bathroom, boy, counselor, girls', homework, liar, library, list, monster, office, school, teacher, toilet; List 3 = birthday, book, candles, frown, heart, letter, love, party, presents, punch, ribbon, singing, smile, star; Total list = Andy, Bartholomew, basketball, bathroom, birthday, book, boy, Bradley, candles, Carla, Chalkers, Claudia, Colleen, counselor, Davis, Fishkin, frown, girls', heart, homework, Jeff, letter, liar, library, list, Lori, love, Melinda, monster, Mrs. Ebbel, office, party, presents, punch, ribbon, Ronnie, school, singing, smile, star, teacher, toilet

Why Mosquitoes Buzz in People's Ears by Verna Aardema
page 149: Picture names from left to right, top to bottom are monkey, crow, mosquito, rabbit, owl, python, lion, and iguana.
page 151: Under the /kw/ like in question column, quake, quiz, square, squeak, quilt, and squid should be listed. Under the /k/ like in mosquito column, opaque, unique, bouquet, conquer, and clique should be listed.